FLAPPERS

and the

NEW AMERICAN WOMAN

PERCEPTIONS OF WOMEN FROM 1918 THROUGH THE 1920s

Catherine Gourley

Twenty-First Century Books • Minneapolis

For Catherine Kelley Hannon, whom I never met but know without a doubt that she was a strong-willed new American woman

Text copyright © 2008 by Catherine Gourley

Twenty-First Century Books
A division of Lerner Publishing Group, Inc.
241 First Avenue North
Minneapolis, MN 55401 U.S.A.

Website address: www.lernerbooks.com

Library of Congress Cataloging-in-Publication Data

Gourley, Catherine, 1950–
    Flappers and the new American woman : perceptions of women from 1918 through the 1920s / by Catherine Gourley.
      p.   cm. — (Images and issues of women in the twentieth century)
    Includes bibliographical references and index.
    ISBN 978–0–8225–6060–9 (lib. bdg. : alk. paper)
    1. Women—United States—History—20th century. 2. Women—United States—Social conditions—20th century.
  3. Women—United States—Social life and customs—20th century. 4. Popular culture—United States—History—20th century.
  5. Nineteen twenties. I. Title.
    HQ1420.G67 2008
    305.40973'09042—dc22   2006028983

Manufactured in the United States of America
1 2 3 4 5 6 – JR – 13 12 11 10 09 08

Contents

Women of the 1920s defied the conventions of acceptable female behavior. They expressed their new freedom by smoking in public, shedding their corsets, exposing their legs, and other shocking behavior.

AUTHOR'S NOTE

I never knew my grandmother. Sadly, she died the year I was born. I've seen only a grainy photograph of her seated in a rocking chair holding her granddaughter, my older sister. In this image, Catherine Hannon is an old woman. She has pinned her long, white hair into a bun. She is not smiling. But then life was not always easy for her. She was an immigrant from Ireland, the mother of eleven children. Four of those children would die—two baby daughters from illness and two grown sons in coal mining accidents.

The photograph is only one image I have of her. Other images fill my imagination, planted there by stories my mother has told. Catherine Hannon was a housewife and mother but she also worked outside the home. One of her jobs was as a housekeeper for a county judge. Although she didn't have a college education or a career as a professional woman, I, neverthe-less, think of her as "a new American woman." She voted. She believed women should think for themselves. She was hard working and independent. Once a year, she left her family and traveled alone by train from Wilkes-Barre, Pennsylvania, to Cleveland, Ohio, where she vacationed with family.

THE LADIES'
HOME JOURNAL

FEBRUARY 1921   THE CURTIS PUBLISHING COMPANY PHILADELPHIA   20 CENTS

A woman entering the second decade of the twentieth century was about to leave her pedestal. Some willingly jumped off to become the era's unconventional young women known as flappers. Others cautiously stepped into the lifestyle of the new, independent American woman.

She needed the time for herself, she told my mother. Every woman needs to take care of herself as well as her family.

An image can be visual, such as a photograph, a painting, or a film. But images are also print documents, including letters, diaries, newspaper articles, short stories, and novels. In researching this book, the second in a series on women's images and issues, I traveled back in time and studied other photographs of other women—some young and some old, like my grandmother. I read newspapers and old magazines, including a copy of my grandmother's *Good Housekeeping* from April 1924. I listened to gravelly broadcasts of old radio programs. Specifically, I hunted for answers to two questions: How did the popular media of the past portray women? Were those images of women accurate or misleading? In doing so, I discovered more about my grandmother. I returned to the present day with a better understanding of what her life might have been like. Surely,

many of the dreams and disappointments of women in the 1920s were much the same as those my grandmother had.

Throughout the twentieth century, media images—whether fact or fiction, stereotypical or sensationalized—influenced women's perception of themselves. But the influence was not always blind acceptance. Many women rebelled against the images society had painted for them. Their rebellion not only made headlines but also opened doors for other women to express their own individuality. As you read, you, too, will travel back in time. I hope you'll return to the present with greater understanding of how popular culture may have influenced your mother, your grandmother, perhaps even your great-grandmother. More important, I hope you'll see yourself reflected within these pages and understand that you—not society—holds the paintbrush that creates the person you become.

—*Catherine Gourley*

a prologue
*a*rmistice day, november 11, 1918

Women were the guardians of morality; they were made of finer stuff than men and were expected to act accordingly. Young girls must look forward in innocence . . . to a romantic love match which would lead them to the altar and to living happily-ever-after; and until the "right man" came along they must allow no male to kiss them. . . . [World War I] had not long been over when cries of alarm from parents, teachers and [clergy] began to rend the air. For the boys and girls just growing out of adolescence were making mincemeat of this code.

—Frederick Lewis Allen, *Only Yesterday*, writing about the 1920s

the sirens began wailing before dawn.

Church bells rang. From railroad yards and factory buildings, steam whistles blasted the air. In cities across the United States—Oneonta, New York; Fort Collins, Colorado; Portland, Oregon—families woke to the same riot of noise. They stumbled from their beds and peered through the windows. Some dressed hurriedly in the dark to join their neighbors who had already gathered in the streets. "Is it true?" they asked. "Are they certain?"

There were no computers, televisions, or radios in 1918 to confirm the news. Official information came over telegraph wires to government offices and news agencies. And so the crowds began to move toward the downtown sections of their cities. There in the newsrooms, copy editors were busily rewriting the day's headlines to read: "War Ends; Germany Surrenders; Armistice Signed."

For the past four years, a world war had destroyed much of Europe. Millions of people had died, including more than one hundred thousand U.S. soldiers. Then on the eleventh day of the eleventh month, in a railroad car somewhere in France, the leaders of the warring armies had at last signed the peace treaty. Yes, said the mayors of the cities. Yes, said the newspaper publishers. It is official. The Great War is over. (Following the end of World War II [1939–1945], the Great War became known as World War I [1914–1918].)

The noise grew louder. People whooped and cheered. The mostly well-to-do families who owned automobiles cranked up their engines and rode through the streets, honking their horns and dragging tin cans. Others grabbed pots and pans, cowbells, and saw blades—anything to bang or clang or whiz and whistle. In Portland, Oregon, a woman wound up her alarm clock and let it ring, then wound it up again and again and again.

In November 1918, American women danced in the streets during the celebration marking the end of World War I. Ordinarily, young ladies did not behave so wildly in public, but this was Armistice Day! Facing page: Headlines tell of the end of World War I, November 11, 1918.

In New York City, the girls at Barnard College snake-danced down the avenue, one behind the other, each with her hands on the hips of the girl in front of her. Their unusual behavior was just part of the spontaneous joy everyone felt.

No one went back to bed. This would be a day of celebration unlike any other in the country's history.

If you were a young woman living in the United States on this day, surely you would have joined the celebration. You would have pulled on your wool stockings and buttoned your boots. You would have pinned up your long hair—your hair most certainly was long, because short hair on a woman was shocking if not immoral! You would have put on a hat and gloves, and your skirt would have hidden all but your boot-covered ankles. Outside, you'd have laughed and paraded through the streets with everyone else. The cold air, not cosmetics, would rouge your cheeks, for a proper young lady did not wear makeup or paint her lips. If a young man should suddenly hug you out of sheer excitement, well . . . you could excuse his boldness in touching you, given the wonderful occasion that peace had returned to the world.

If you were a single woman who worked in an office building, you might have spent the morning hours leaning from the window to watch the merry-making below. You would have torn up whatever paper you could find into confetti and let it fly like snow from the windows. When you ran out of paper, you might have showered a fine mist of talcum powder on the revelers below. By noon you would have joined them. Across the country, factories, offices, and restaurants shut down to celebrate the end of the war.

The well-dressed young women of 1918 could not even imagine what the fashions of the next decade would have in store.

In Pennsylvania, Philadelphians came out in huge numbers on November 11, 1918, to celebrate the ending of the Great War.

In New York City, mobs blocked the passage of automobiles and horse-drawn wagons. There were no traffic lights in 1918. They would come years later. Instead, a police officer attempted to direct traffic from a metal tower in the street, but the people—and horses—were too excited to pay much attention to him.

Parades formed on every corner and marched up streets and down. In Oneonta the parade included a coffin and a stuffed scarecrow, meant to represent the kaiser, or leader, of Germany. The people cheered as the men hung the dummy from the clock tower on a downtown building. In Fort Collins, people called their stuffed dummy of the German ruler Bill the Beast, and it too hung on public display. Throughout the day, men released their pent-up fury over the war by firing buckshot into the dummy as it swung at the end of its rope.

Even as evening approached, the partying continued. People dragged crates from store alleys and warehouses to build bonfires. Flames brightened the night skies in numerous cities. Voices joined in song.

They belted out this verse, which had been so popular during the war:

> What's the use of worrying?
> It never was worth while, so
> Pack up your troubles in your old
> kit-bag,
> And smile, smile, smile.

People all around the world—in Canada, Great Britain, and Australia—were celebrating Armistice Day in much the same way as the Americans were. For one day, the world truly packed up its troubles and smiled.

The next day, the fires were smoldering embers. The street cleaners began sweeping away the snowbanks of confetti. The cities and towns did not look much different from a few days ago, and yet somehow the world had changed. This had been "the war to end all wars." But could peace really last? People wanted to forget the horrors of sniper's bullets, whistling bombs, and poisonous mustard gas. But it was not easy. The war had destroyed too many lives. In the weeks and months that followed, war veterans returned, though some were crippled and without limbs. The world could never return to the way life had been before the killing and the maiming of so many men.

If you were a woman living in the United States on this morning after Armistice Day, you might not have sensed a difference. But change was in the air all the same. A cultural revolution was about to seize the country in much the same way as the Armistice Day celebrations had erupted in cities from coast to coast. The United States was entering the age of modernism and mass advertising. Industrial innovations were changing the way the country worked and played. New inventions, such as the wireless radiophone, would change communications. More and more ordinary families, not just the well-to-do, purchased telephones and automobiles. Electricity illuminated city streets. Modern times had arrived!

the world could never return to the way life had been before the killing and the maiming of so many men.

In the decade to come, women, in particular, would experience new freedoms, including the right to vote. They would change how they dressed and wore their hair. These daughters would challenge their mother's old-fashioned ideas of morality too. As young women's attitudes about dating and marriage changed, so did their behavior. The young woman who on Armistice Day pulled

The advent of electricity, kitchen appliances, and the automobile introduced ordinary women of the 1920s and 1930s to a whole new concept: leisure time. Games such as bridge and maj-jongg (above) sprang into vogue.

on her wool stockings and blushed at a young man's hug would be almost unrecognizable by the end of the 1920s.

The media mirrored these cultural changes and the choices women made. Images of flappers and the new American woman began to appear in advertisements, movies, and on the radio. The flapper cut her hair, slipped into a shapeless, short dress, and danced all night. The new American woman might not have dressed in such a shocking style, but her behavior was just as startling. She appeared on the athletic field and in the workplace and made headlines for achievements (and sometimes dangerous stunts) that would have been unheard of in the years before the Great War.

Flappers and the New American Woman is the second volume in a series of books that journey back in time to explore how popular cultures of the twentieth century—advertisements, books, film, radio, newspapers, and magazines—portrayed women, and how women, in turn, changed the way the world perceived them.

Chapter One

Modern Girls and the Media

She will never make you a hatband or knit a necktie, but she'll drive you from the station [on] hot summer nights in her own little sport car. She'll don knickers [knee-length trousers] and go skiing with you; or if it happens to be summertime, swimming; she'll dive as well as you, perhaps better.

—Ruth Hooper, *New York Times*, July 16, 1922

On a summer night in 1918,

a young woman waltzed with her dance partner on the veranda of a country club in Montgomery, Alabama. Zelda Sayre was almost but not quite old enough to pin up her hair as young ladies did when they reached the mature age of eighteen. Her father was a much-respected judge in Alabama. Her mother was a southern belle, a proper lady of the upper class. Minnie Sayre had taught her daughters the "no-lady" rules that she herself had learned as a girl. No lady left the house without every button on her gloves fastened. No lady sat with her limbs crossed. (Limbs were legs, but *legs* was a vulgar word in polite society in 1918.)

Zelda Sayre laughed at her mother's old-fashioned ideas. Unlike her mother and even her older sisters, Zelda thought of herself as a modern girl. Young men frequently called on her, but they did not walk up the steps and knock on the door. They arrived in automobiles and pressed on the horn. Quite likely, her gloves—if, in fact, Sayre even wore gloves—were unbuttoned as she dashed out the door to join them.

On this summer night at the country club, young men surrounded Sayre. Each waited for his turn to be her dancing partner. All at once, a stranger walked across the veranda toward her. He tapped the shoulder of the young man with whom she was dancing, cutting in to become her new partner.

Sayre did not object. The stranger was an army lieutenant and very handsome. His name was F. Scott Fitzgerald. Among the "no-lady" rules was this one: "No lady pursues a man. The man must pursue the lady." However, even Emily Post, who wrote books on etiquette, admitted that women were "catlike [and] may do a little stalking." Sayre

Zelda Fitzgerald (above) *was considered by many of her era to be the embodiment of the modern 1920s woman. She actually led the glittering life that her husband F. Scott Fitzgerald* (right) *described in his novels. Several of his most notable characters are said to be based on her.* Facing page: *The car gave women of the 1920s new freedoms.*

was very catlike. She nuzzled her face against the collar of Fitzgerald's uniform. The lieutenant fell in love that night.

In well-to-do families, such as the Sayres, a young lady did not kiss a young man unless they were engaged to be married. This was yet another "no-lady" rule that Sayre broke, especially during the summer that Fitzgerald courted her. Years later, she wrote in her autobiographical novel, *Save Me the Waltz*, about kissing an army officer who very likely was Scott Fitzgerald. He had proposed marriage, but she had turned him down.

"Then why did you kiss me?" he asked.

"Because," she replied, "I had never kissed a man with a moustache before."

Zelda Sayre was a modern woman, and she knew what she wanted. Of course, she would marry, quite possibly the handsome F. Scott Fitzgerald. But before she settled down to become a society wife and mother, she intended to have some fun.

The Outcast and the Ordinary People

Margaret Mead was nothing like Zelda Sayre. Boys did not call on her in automobiles or wait in line to be her dance partner. Her middle-class family did not belong to a country club. Instead, her parents read books of philosophy. Her father was a professor and her mother, too, had taught school before she married. Although money was sometimes tight, Margaret understood that her family was different from "the common herd," as her mother snobbishly called ordinary people.

"Ordinary people let their children chew gum, read girls' and boys' books, drink ice cream sodas, and go to Coney Island [an amusement park in New York]. . . ," Mead wrote. Often Margaret longed for that sort of life. Her mother, however, believed in giving money to worthy causes rather than spending it on frivolous things such as ribbons and bows or household gadgets. Instead of "no-lady" rules, Margaret's mother stressed just one motto by which her children should live: do good because it is right to do good.

When she was sixteen, Margaret kissed a boy for the first time. The boy's name was Luther Cressman. In kissing each other, the couple sealed their engagement to be married. Luther was four years older than Margaret and studying to become a minister. They planned to marry after Margaret graduated from college. Margaret's mother had modern ideas. She thought a woman should be educated. She should have a career and not be dependent on a husband for a living. And so in the autumn of 1919, Margaret left home—and her fiancé—for DePauw University in Indiana.

> "Ordinary people let their children chew gum, read girls' and boys' books, drink ice cream sodas, and go to Coney Island [amusement park]."
>
> —Margaret Mead, writing about the 1920s

Mead had imagined herself as a college girl who sat up all night with other enthusiastic students talking about "things that mattered." But once she arrived on the campus, she discovered that the female students were more interested in social relationships than in social issues. They wore raccoon coats, jumped up and down at football games, and went to sorority parties. These coeds were the "ordinary people" that Mead had envied. Although she hungered for knowledge, she wanted to have fun and make friends too.

The social life at DePauw revolved around sororities and fraternities. A girl did not simply join a sorority. She had to be invited by members of the group. Sorority members held "rushing parties" to meet and

Although she preferred not to be called a feminist, Margaret Mead was a liberated woman and was active in the women's movement of the early 1900s. She felt that all young women should feel free to postpone marriage and family in order to pursue their education and career.

evaluate prospective members. Mead attended her first—and only—rushing party soon after arriving on campus. She wore a dress that she had designed and sewn herself. She described the colorful fabric as "a field of wheat with poppies against a blue sky with white clouds." It was dreadful, she would later admit. At the time, however, she was quite proud of it. When the sorority sisters saw her in the garish gown, they turned their backs on her. The message was clear. They did not want her. "I was confronted, for the first time in my life, with being thoroughly unacceptable to almost everyone and on grounds in which I had previously been taught to take pride," she said.

Mead was an outsider. Being rejected from "society" helped her to see more clearly the person she did *not* want to become: a wife who was a helpmate only, a woman in good standing with the community garden club. Like Zelda Sayre, Margaret Mead was a modern girl—but Mead's interests were not automobiles, raccoon coats, summer dances, or kisses from men with mustaches.

> Being rejected from "society" helped Mead to see more clearly the person she did not want to become: a wife who was a helpmate only, a woman in good standing with the community garden club.

Mead was so unhappy at DePauw University that she left after one year. She transferred to Barnard College in New York City. Here she found the intellectual excitement she had craved. After graduation, she married the Reverend Luther Cressman. But she kept her own name rather than taking his. This was a bold move, and it would not be her last. She became an anthropologist. Few women studied to be this type of social scientist. Those who did worked in the quiet and safe spaces of research libraries. Mead wanted none of that. She intended to travel to faraway places and to mingle with real people.

Coney Island on a Summer Day

On a summer Sunday afternoon, "the ordinary people" that Margaret Mead's mother preferred not to mingle with gathered on the beach on Coney Island. Most were immigrants or the sons and daughters of immigrants. They spoke in many different languages—Polish, Greek, Russian, and Italian. They stood in lines to ride the roller coasters and other amusement park rides, including the Wonder Wheel, rising 150 feet (45 meters) in the air. On a single summer day, reported Bruce Bliven in 1921 in the *New Republic,* fourteen thousand people changed their clothes in the bathhouses and waded into the surf of the Atlantic Ocean.

For working girls who couldn't afford any other kind of vacation, Coney Island offered hours of fun. In 1920 they could ride the subway from Manhattan, New York, to the park for just a nickel. Once there, a girl might convince a fellow to buy her a hot dog at Nathan's and take her for a ride on the roller coaster. If they had a few extra nickels, they might stop and gawk at the sideshows that featured the amazing spider boy, the tattooed lady, or a fire-eater and a sword swallower. Or they might wander through the wax museum. Coney Island was "cheap pleasure for cheap people," a visitor from France commented.

"New Yorkers of the better sort," wrote Bliven in 1921, viewed Coney Island as "garish and soiled." Still, he loved its garishness and the river of humanity that flowed along its wide plank boardwalk. At night, he said, when the festoons of electric lights came to life, Coney Island was a magical place.

When public transportation made Brooklyn's Coney Island (left) accessible to the masses, thousands of people crowded the beaches on summer days. In 1920, if a woman's bathing costume did not include a skirt or pantaloons, the police would remove her from the beach.

Margaret Mead ignored the dangers of traveling to the remote Pacific islands of Samoa in order to study family life there. Throughout her life, Mead would continue to visit the island nations in the South Pacific. She is pictured above on a trip to Bali, Indonesia, in 1957.

The faraway place she chose was Samoa, a string of islands in the South Pacific. Here she could study native families and children. Her friends and fellow scientists tried to dissuade her. The dangers of these remote islands included cannibalism and tropical diseases. Many male anthropologists had died on such missions. For a young woman to travel to this "uncivilized" corner of the world—especially without her husband—was simply shocking. Mead was headstrong. In 1925 she sailed for Hawaii and from there to Samoa. The book she would write upon her return would challenge society's understanding of youth and culture and make her a world-famous social scientist.

The Brooklyn Bonfire and the Silver Screen

Not all modern girls were from middle-class families or upper-crust society. Nor were they all college educated. Some were poor. Many never attended high school. Instead, they worked long hours in factories, dime stores, or laundries. Their families depended on their income to survive. But these girls, too, could be rebellious and independent. And they, too, had dreams.

In New York City, fifteen-year-old Clara Bow sat in a dark movie house. The screen that loomed before her was a window to another world far away from the crowded tenement building where she lived. Clara's childhood was bleak. Her mother suffered from a mental illness. Her father was an alcoholic who sometimes beat Clara. Through motion pictures, Clara said she discovered beauty in the world: "distant lands, lovely homes, romance, nobility, glamour." Every penny she saved was for one purpose only—to return to that other world of the silver screen.

Mary Pickford was her favorite actress. She had long blonde curls and wore ruffled dresses. The characters she played were kind and loving, very different from Clara's mother. As the images flickered in the dark movie house, Clara stitched a silver dream for herself. One day she, too, would become a star. She told no one of her dream, especially not her mother, who'd laugh at Clara, telling her yet again that she wasn't pretty or clever enough to be a success at anything. She believed her mother when she told her she wasn't pretty. Clara's hair was red—too red, she thought, to be attractive. Often she pretended to be someone else. She would put on her mother's old skirts and sweaters.

Mary Pickford was the most popular as well as the most prolific star of the silent film era. In 1909 she actually appeared in fifty-one films. Later, she went on to star in Hollywood sound films, becoming the first female actor to earn more than one million dollars per year.

Lucille's New Name

By 1931 the silent film era had ended with the introduction of movies with sound, known as the talkies. Audiences who had once loved to look at—and look like—Clara Bow weren't as interested in her anymore. Moviegoers were growing tired of It girls. ("It" was a coded reference to sex appeal.) Other stars in Hollywood were glowing more brightly, including the auburn-haired, blue-eyed Lucille LeSueur.

In 1925 Metro-Goldwyn-Mayer (MGM) studios introduced LeSueur to movie fans across the country. The studio announced in *Movie Weekly* a nationwide contest inviting fans to give the eighteen-year-old LeSueur a new name to use on-screen. "I think Hollywood is the most beautiful place in the world," the starlet told the readers of *Movie Weekly*. She added that her happiness would be complete once the readers chose her new screen name.

The name chosen was Joan Crawford. LeSueur hated it, though she admitted it was easier to pronounce. MGM gave her more than a new name. As with Clara Bow and all movie stars of the times, the studio publicity department created a reputation for their new starlet and selected roles for her to play. Frequently, Joan Crawford portrayed showgirls in the big city who aspired to marry a man with money. "Her Charleston (a popular dance) was

Joan Crawford poses in a stage costume and ballet shoes in 1925, the year MGM launched her on what was to be a forty-year career in film.

hotter, her gowns tighter than any other's in Hollywood," wrote a reporter in *Life* magazine.

Like Clara Bow, Joan Crawford's image appeared in hundreds of magazines. But unlike Clara Bow, Joan Crawford's star did not fade. In the talkies of the 1930s, she took on more serious and diverse roles. Gone was the showgirl image. She told *Photoplay* magazine in 1937, "I want really to be a very great actress. I'm willing to work hard to do it. I'm ready to give years of my life."

She did. Lucille LeSueur starred in eighty movies over a career that lasted decades until her death in 1969.

Then standing in front of a mirror, she imitated the expressions Mary Pickford made in the movies.

One day Clara read about the "Fame and Fortune" contest in a movie magazine. The announcement stressed that the aspiring actress who won must have personality and acting ability as well as beauty. The young woman selected would have a small role in a soon-to-be-made movie. To enter, however, Clara had to send her photograph to the magazine. A photograph cost a dollar, and all her saved pennies weren't enough. She went to the only person who would not laugh at her. A dollar was a great deal of money for Clara's father. But he gave it to her just the same—or so Clara would later claim in a fan magazine story about her early life.

Clara didn't like the photograph of herself, but she mailed it anyway. Then she waited. Hundreds of girls all across the United States might enter the contest. What chance could she possibly have? Still, hope filled her heart. For weeks she could think of nothing else. Then, at last, an envelope arrived. With cold, shaking fingers, Clara opened it and read that she had won.

As the contest winner, Clara Bow made her first appearance on the silver screen in 1923. She played Dot Morgan, "a sad-eyed" stowaway aboard a whaling ship in *Down to the Sea in Ships*. A year later, the Western

Association of Motion Picture Advertisers (WAMPAS) selected her as one of their "baby stars." The baby stars weren't babies at all but rather young actresses whom the advertisers believed would surely rise to stardom.

Traditionally, a diva is a female opera star. During the modern times of the 1920s, the phrase took on a different connotation.

Thousands of young women imitated Clara Bow. They copied her short hairstyle with cheek curls. They rimmed their eyes with dark kohl makeup. They learned how to make her Cupid's bow lips: paint the lips with white makeup, dip a thumb in a cake of red paint, and then press two thumbprints on the upper lip and one thumbprint below.

Women Make News in 1929: The Teenage Aviatrix

The most famous woman pilot of the 1920s and 1930s was undoubtedly Amelia Earhart. She had short, curly hair and wore pants and a leather jacket when flying. But Earhart wasn't the only woman pilot who risked her life to set and break aviation records.

Elinor Smith was just fifteen when she flew solo for the first time. At sixteen she became the youngest woman to earn her pilot's license. On January 20, 1929, the seventeen-year-old pilot roared into the sky hoping to set a new solo endurance flying record. The existing record was twelve hours. She intended to fly eighteen hours nonstop, circling New York City.

The cockpit of her biplane (an early airplane with two sets of wings) was open to the frigid air. She had rubbed a layer of cold cream on her face to protect it from the wind, and she wore a mask made of a soft chamois cloth. Goggles protected her eyes, but the glass kept fogging. To protect her hands, she wore fur-lined gloves—but the night air still numbed her fingers. To stay awake—and warm—she sang aloud "every song she could remember."

Her greatest challenge wasn't the cold. Nor was it the leg cramps from being strapped inside the cockpit for so many hours. What frightened Smith the most was landing at night. She had never done that before. She had no airport spotlights or runway flares. She had to rely on her eyesight and the feel of the plane as she glided down.

A diva was an attractive and often temperamental woman. The growing popularity not only of moving pictures but also of fan magazines and tabloid newspapers helped to make Clara Bow a diva of the silent screen. The media christened her the Brooklyn Bonfire because of her flaming hair. What Bow had was sex appeal, but even in the modern 1920s, that was a shocking term.

Even the tabloid newspapers that specialized in scandals and sensational stories couldn't use the term openly. So they gave her another nickname: It girl.

Clara Bow played dozens of characters in the years that followed. The characters' stories and circumstances differed, but their basic type did not. They were hard-boiled (tough) modern girls who cared

In 1928 Elinor Smith set a light plane altitude record of 11,889 feet (3,624 m), just one of many records she was to set during her career. In 1929 alone she set four world records.

Any misjudgment and she'd crash. If the crash didn't kill her, then the exploding fuel tanks might.

At three thirty in the morning, unable to fight her exhaustion any longer, Smith landed safely. Despite the mask, her face was chafed raw. Her legs were stiff, and she was sore. But she had set a new endurance record of twelve hours, sixteen minutes, and forty-five seconds. The media published her photograph and tagged her the Flying Flapper.

Soon after, Smith began planning still another flying feat, another record to beat. Two years earlier, Charles Lindbergh had become the first man to fly solo across the Atlantic Ocean to Paris, France. Maybe she'd fly nonstop to Rome, Italy, she told a reporter.

Said her mother, "Try and stop her!"

little for old-fashioned morals. Reporter Adela Rogers St. Johns believed Clara Bow had real talent, more so than even Mary Pickford. But Paramount Studios insisted on casting Bow in the same character role in movie after movie—the sexy It girl.

During the 1920s, Bow's star continued to rise, but what the media and the movie studios create, they can also destroy. As the decade ended, the popular press, which had launched and then rode on Bow's rising star, began to pull her down. The tabloids, in particular, were cruel. Headlines revealed details of her private life. She had multiple love affairs, the tabloids reported. She gambled and lost thousands of dollars. She drank. Some of the stories were outright lies, intended simply to sell newspapers. Also, publicity men at Paramount Studios wrote many of the exaggerated stories and gave them to the press as a way to boost ticket sales for Bow's movies.

Perhaps the stress of becoming an international star so quickly at such a young age wore down Clara Bow. The movie screen was no longer a place of beauty and nobility for her. Instead, Paramount Studios had taken advantage of her by promoting her "crisis-a-day" reputation. In June 1931, *Time* reported that Clara Bow had suffered a nervous breakdown. On her own request, she terminated her contract with the movie studio.

Clara Bow's silver star had fallen.

The Original Radio Girls

Divas of film ruled the silver screen. But another popular entertainment was rapidly invading U.S. homes—the wireless radiophone. One day in January 1920, singer Vaughn DeLeath stepped inside a tiny studio, not much bigger than a closet. She leaned toward the microphone and began singing "Swanee River" in a low crooning voice. Because that song was perhaps the first-ever sung by a woman over a "wireless," Vaughn DeLeath earned the nickname the Original Radio Girl.

In the earliest days of radio, people built their own radio sets using their knowledge of mathematics and carpentry. Boys, but not girls, typically studied these subjects in school. Most science and hobby magazines about radios, therefore, pictured boys tinkering with the new technology while girls sat wide eyed and listened.

Vaughn DeLeath, shown here in a sheet music inset, called herself the First Lady of Radio. At one point, she sued singer Kate Smith for using the same name. DeLeath won.

A Girl Radio Girl

Perhaps the first woman to be both an announcer and an engineer was Eunice Randall (later, Eunice Randall Thompson). At the age of nineteen, she was broadcasting on 1XE, a radio station operated from studios on the campus of Tufts College in Boston, Massachusetts.

To Boston radio fans of the early 1920s, Eunice Randall was the Story Lady. Two nights a week from late 1921 through 1923, she had a sponsored program (the station's first—sponsored by *Little Folks* magazine), reading stories to children. She also did the police reports, gave Morse code practice, sometimes announced the news, and when guests didn't show up, she and one of the station's engineers would sing duets! She even became the assistant chief announcer. 1XE (which was renamed WGI in February of 1922) was heard all over the United States, and Randall received fan mail (and more than a few marriage proposals) from many different cities.

Eunice Randall was as involved in amateur radio as she was in professional broadcasting. She built her own ham (amateur with a special license) station and ultimately became one of the first women in New England to hold the first class license.

Women Make News in 1923: Vincent's Voice

Edna St. Vincent Millay was turning heads and stealing the spotlight long before she won the Pulitzer Prize in Poetry in 1923. From a young age, she was destined for literary fame. At fourteen she won her first award for poetry from *St. Nicholas* magazine. At seventeen her poem "Renascence" was published in a poetry anthology, *The Lyric Year.*

"I want, and have always wanted—dreadfully—to go to college," she wrote in a letter to the editor of the magazine. That published poem helped her to win a scholarship to Vassar College in New York. Even before she had graduated from college, she published her first book of poetry.

The lady poet preferred to call herself Vincent. (Her middle name was in honor of St. Vincent's Hospital in New York City,

Edna St. Vincent Millay, 1933

where her uncle's life had been saved just before she was born.) In her poetry, she expressed a passionate belief that women should have control of their own bodies, minds, and pocketbooks. "I want to write so that those who read me will say . . . 'Life can be exciting and free and intense.' I really mean it!"

She wrote too about social and political injustices. In 1927 the state of Massachusetts planned to execute Bartolomeo Vanzetti and Nicola Sacco, two Italian immigrants whom a jury had found guilty of murder. Although another man had confessed to the crime, the court refused to free or even hold a new trial for Sacco and Vanzetti. Along with other angry men and women, Vincent marched on the streets of Boston, where the men were imprisoned. She carried a sign that read: "If These Men Are Executed, Justice Is Dead in Massachusetts." The police arrested her. She refused to pay the fine to avoid going to jail. She had done no wrong, she argued. She was exercising her right of free speech. On April 22, the *New York World* published a poem she had written about the Sacco and Vanzetti case. "Evil does overwhelm/The larkspur and the corn," she said in her verse.

Hours later, just past midnight on April 23, the immigrants were put to death by electrocution. Neither Vincent's protests nor her poetry could save them, but this new American woman had made her voice heard.

Within two years of DeLeath's radio debut, however, a "broadcasting boom" swept the nation. As more and more stations began broadcasting, doors of opportunity opened for women. Some, like DeLeath, were entertainers who sang and played instruments. Others found jobs as producers, coming up with ideas for new programs and hiring the performers. Others took jobs as writers and still others as announcers. A few even learned the technology to work the radio transmitters.

One of the most popular radio programs of the 1920s, *The Man in the Moon*, was aimed at children. The first broadcast was over station WJZ in Newark, New Jersey. The announcer told the listening audience, "The radiophone, which is the wireless, has made it possible for the Man in the Moon to talk to you." The idea of the moon transmitting radio signals sparked the imaginations of children throughout the city. The radio engineers used special effects, such as the sound of glass breaking, to suggest that the man in the moon truly had come down to Earth through a window in the roof to read them a different bedtime story in each episode.

The author of these children's stories was Josephine Lawrence, a newspaper reporter for the *Newark Sunday Call*. In addition to her newspaper column on household tips for women, Lawrence wrote many children's books, especially for girls. Her "man in the moon" stories were the first-ever broadcast for children over the wireless, making her an original radio girl too.

At first, the radio producer encouraged Lawrence to read her stories herself—but she refused. The radio transmitter was on the top floor of a factory building in Newark, New Jersey. The only way to reach the rooftop studio was by climbing a 15-foot (4.5 m) iron ladder. That was a little too close to the moon for Lawrence. And there might have been another reason for her refusal. The writer was painfully shy. Although her radio listeners would not be able to see her, she preferred to have the fanciful "man in the moon" as the teller of her stories.

The Literary Ladies

Moving picture shows, radio broadcasts, tabloid newspapers, and fan magazines— these were the media of modern times. But the new American Woman was leaving her mark in another area of communication as well: best-selling novels.

In 1921 Edith Wharton became the first woman novelist to win literature's coveted Pulitzer Prize. Her 1920 novel *The Age of Innocence* gave readers a peek into the world of New York's upper-crust society in the 1870s. Newland Archer, the main character, falls in love with the Countess Ellen Olenska, but her reputation is stained. And so Newland marries a respectable woman he does not love, for that is the type of wife society expects him to have.

The novel was historical fiction. Edith Wharton was writing about the past. The respectable women in her novel were much like Zelda Sayre's mother. They followed the "no-lady" rules. Fifty years had passed, however. Perhaps many of Edith Wharton's present-day readers saw her story of lost love as a warning. Modern men and women would not make the same mistakes as their parents or grandparents had. They would not sacrifice true love for social acceptance.

In Edna Ferber's 1924 novel *So Big,* main character Selina DeJong is a farmer's wife. She is "a young woman in a blue calico dress, faded and earth-grimed," the author wrote. Her hands, too, are "crusted and inground with the soil." DeJong has big ideas for how her husband might modernize the farm. But he refuses to change. When an accident takes his life, Selina has to rely on her own sensibilities and strengths to survive and provide a future for her son.

> Women and men of the 1920s would not sacrifice true love for social acceptance.

In the 1920s, families were leaving their farms and moving into towns and cities. It was still another sign of modern times—the United States was becoming more urban. And so many women who read *So Big* in 1925 would have understood DeJong's struggles and found courage in her success as a modern woman.

Author Julia Peterkin, on the other hand, had grown up in the South, among the Gullah people, who are descended from the African slaves brought to Georgia and South Carolina. Her father was a physician. Her mother died when she was very young, and a black nurse had raised her. As a young woman, she married a wealthy plantation owner who employed hundreds of African Americans. When she was forty years old, Peterkin began writing. That was somewhat unusual for a

Edith Wharton (far left) *started a trend. Of the nine Pulitzer Prizes awarded for fiction in the 1920s, five went to female novelists. In addition to Edith Wharton, Willa Cather* (second from left), *Margaret Wilson, Edna Ferber* (second from right), *and Julia Peterkin* (far right) *won the honor. The settings and the characters of their novels differed. But each writer, in her own way, questioned a woman's place in the home and in society.*

southern woman of means. What was truly shocking, however, were the kind of stories she told. She wrote about the Gullah people with whom she had grown up. Why? Her answer was simple: "I have lived among the Negroes. I like them. They are my friends, and I have learned so much from them."

Even more shocking was how she portrayed her characters—in a sympathetic and realistic way rather than as racial stereotypes. African American educator W. E. B. DuBois once said of Julia Peterkin, "She is a Southern white woman, but she has the eye and the ear to see beauty and know truth." *Scarlet Sister May,* her novel that won the Pulitzer Prize in 1929, was about a young black woman who marries at sixteen and whose husband leaves her. The novel por-trays Mary as a hardworking woman, whose toil in the fields kept her body lean and strong. As the author described her:

> *She could swing an ax and cut the toughest wood for hours at a time without a taint of weariness. She could jerk a hoe day after day through the hottest sunshine. She could pick cotton with the best and come home at night as cheerful and fresh as when she waked at dawn.*

A Woman's Glory

Margaret Mead spoke for herself and the other female students at Barnard College when she said, "We belonged to a generation of young women who felt extraordinarily free—free from the demand to marry unless we chose to do so, free to postpone marriage while we did other things, free from the need to bargain and hedge that had burdened and restricted women of earlier generations. We laughed at the idea that a woman could be an old maid at the age of twenty-five."

Whether married or single, rich or poor, an actress or aviatrix, a social scientist or award-winning writer, modern girls were making headlines. But surely not every American woman in the 1920s laughed at the idea of being an old maid at twenty-five. Not all American women were modern girls. Or were they?

Newspaper columnist Josephine Lawrence decided to find out. She invited the readers of the *Newark Sunday Call* to write a letter on the topic of "Why I Am Glad I Am a Woman." The newspaper would award a one-dollar cash prize to the five best letters submitted. She wrote:

> *Probably at some time in her life every woman has fervently wished she might have been born a man. A few of us may suffer from chronic envy, but, except for a few brief—and generally youthful—flare-ups, women accept their sex philosophically and even appreciatively. It isn't such a bad thing to be after all—just a woman. Now is it?*

In her column a week later, Josephine reported on the many letters she had received. The great majority believed that marriage and motherhood was still a "woman's glory."

Modern times had come to the United States. And yet, for every new American woman such as Zelda Sayre, Clara Bow, Margaret Mead, and Julia Peterkin, just as many women did not embrace modern times. Perhaps they agreed with Paul Geraldy, who wrote in *Vogue* magazine in the 1920s, "It is an absolute fact that life, knowledge, and education do not enhance a woman's charm. Quite the contrary!"

> "We belonged to a generation of young women who felt extraordinarily free—free from the demand to marry unless we chose to do so, free to postpone marriage while we did other things, free from the need to bargain and hedge that had burdened and restricted women of earlier generations."
>
> —Margaret Mead

"Is the New Woman a Traitor to Her Race?" asked the *New York Times* in 1921. The article quoted a professor Samuel J. Holmes as stating that women who attend college develop interests in careers rather than children. This was harming the race, the professor argued, because these intelligent women would make the best mothers. The professor noted with alarm that the birthrate was dropping and believed this was the result of more women entering the professions. Even more alarming was the fact that so-called "spinsters" were enjoying their freedom. They no longer sat home alone and sewed. They were out and about and happy.

Perhaps the hullabaloo over women's careers and independence was just a passing fad of the decade known as the Roaring Twenties. In time, these modern girls might come to their senses. They might put down their pens, pilot's goggles, radio microphones, and college textbooks. They'd discard the scandalous tabloids and movie magazines. But not yet.

Throughout the 1920s, the modern girl remained the media's darling.

CHAPTER TWO

Happy Housewives

and

Delicate Women

Advertisements suggested women's greatest achievements were a contented husband, clean children, and delicacy in all matters of personal grooming.

A 1929 advertisement for Amolin deodorizing powder (right) makes it clear that society won't tolerate athlete's foot or embarassing body odor.

Society simply *won't* stand for Indelicate Women

As quick as a wink, a few sprinkles of Amolin will guard your freshness and wholesomeness all day long!

AS SOON as you step from your bath, while the delicious glow of the towel is still upon you, throw under your arms a light coating of Amolin.

For Amolin is a delicate deodorizer *sans reproche*. It does not cover up odors but absorbs them as they arise all day long! It is the clean, fastidious way of disbarring from society the slightest trace of offensive personal odor.

Without smothering the natural function of the pores to exhale impurities, Amolin actually counteracts the odors as soon as they are formed. And it protects, rather than harms, your silken underclothes.

This Personal Deodorant has many uses

There are many uses of this wonderful, scientific powder! Use it after your bath, sprinkle it, if you wish, into your lingerie as you dress, put it in your slippers—you can be free with its use for it is harmless and not at all costly! It is pleasant to smell—but its odor is gone as soon as it touches you! For the great point of Amolin is that it does not cover up one odor with another, but that it neutralizes all personal odors as they arise!

So, go dancing, go shopping, swing your arms in golf or tennis, do a day's work in a hot office, for Amolin used after your bath or sprinkled in your underclothes will protect you all day long! *It is a luxurious and important necessity to dry the body and take away the sticky odor that comes from sea bathing.*

1 *Always use Amolin under the arms when dressing for any social activity*

2 *The most fastidious women use Amolin after the bath all over the body*

3 *Amolin protects delicate lingerie and keeps elastic girdles fresh*

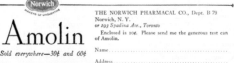

Amolin
Sold everywhere—30¢ and 60¢

THE NORWICH PHARMACAL CO., Dept. B 79
Norwich, N. Y.
or *193 Spadina Ave., Toronto*

Enclosed is 10¢. Please send me the generous test can of Amolin.

Name..................

Address..................

ONE OF THE SOCIAL ISSUES OF THE 1920s

was not whether women should work. Instead, the debate was over why women worked and what they might do with the money they earned.

During the Great War, men left their jobs on farms, in factories, and in offices to become soldiers. Out of necessity, women took their place. They plowed. They spun fabric. They sat at desks and answered telephones, took dictation, and figured costs and expenses. After the war ended and the soldiers returned home, many women gave up their jobs—but not all. In the year after the war ended, approximately one in every four women in the United States worked outside the home. War had opened doors of opportunity for women in the labor force. But women's opportunities were still limited. Most women held traditionally "feminine" jobs. They worked as housemaids, cooks, secretaries, and nurses. Female physicians or dentists or women in professions such as law, science, and business were few and far between.

In 1920 the U.S. Congress passed the Nineteenth Amendment. This amendment gave women the right to vote. That same year, Congress created a Women's Bureau in the Department of Labor. The mission of the new government agency was to set standards and write policies to promote the welfare of wage-earning women, to improve their working conditions, and to recommend changes.

The silent movies showed well-dressed, attractive women enjoying challenging work in offices (top). But in reality, the jobs open to women were more often in factories where long hours and repetitive and sometimes even dangerous work was the norm. The bottom photo shows a shoe factory in Syracuse, New York, in the 1920s.

Women's hopes soared. "At last, after centuries of disabilities and discrimination," said labor leader Margaret Dreier Robins, "women are coming into the labor and festival of life on equal terms with men."

Equal terms meant equal job opportunities and equal pay. Or so the new American woman thought.

She was wrong.

POCKETBOOK PROBLEMS

After numerous investigations, the Women's Bureau announced in a bold headline in all capital letters: "WOMEN RECEIVE MUCH LOWER PAY THAN MEN." The report that followed explained that the difference in wages between men and women was often greater than 50 percent. For example, in 1924 in factories in New York State, men on the average earned $31.50 a week. Women in the same factory earned just $17.50. Likewise, men who manufactured women's clothing earned $46.50 while women earned $26.00. The difference in wages was found in all industries and places of employment—in offices and department stores as well as in factories, the Women's Bureau reported.

The Nineteenth Amendment gave women the right to vote, but it did not force employers to treat or pay women the same way they did men. Why women earned less than men was a complicated issue, even for the researchers in the Women's Bureau. Some employers argued that men and women worked at different tasks requiring different skills. And that was why they paid men more than they paid women. While that may be true, the Women's Bureau discovered another reason: women were less likely to organize as a group and

The Nineteenth Amendment gave women the right to vote, but it did not force employers to treat or pay women the same way they did men.

demand higher wages for themselves.

There were other explanations for unequal wages as well, including what the Women's Bureau researchers called the pin money theory. According to the pin money theory, most women's wages were supplemental—or secondary to the wages earned by the man of the household and thus could be used for frivolous purchases. But investigations by the Women's Bureau proved this theory false. In fact, 90 percent of women who worked did so not to purchase ribbons and bows or to go to movies but to put food on their tables. Their income wasn't pin money at all. Instead, it was necessary to their family's survival. These women were usually from lower-class households where women's and even children's income were needed to put food on the table. The theory of pin money was a myth.

The Women's Bureau was a fact-finding agency only. The bureau had no authority to enforce its recommendations. So despite the bureau's findings, women's wages remained far below men's throughout the 1920s and 1930s and into later decades. Because of the stereotype of women (especially middle-class women) as pin money workers, most employers—and even the working women themselves—viewed women's jobs as temporary.

Popular media continued to reflect the pin money myth through short stories published in women's magazines such as *Good Housekeeping* and in advice books written specifically for young women. In 1924 *Good Housekeeping* published an article titled "Your Daughter and Her Job." The article stated that young ladies who remained in their fathers' homes and engaged in domestic pursuits—baking and sewing, for example—were well prepared for the future. The author wrote that such women were "following normal biological and social instincts which end in mating and mothering." In contrast, working girls risked losing their "domestic instincts" and their "feminine interests." They would fail at becoming good wives and mothers.

"It is unfair to implant in a girl's mind the thought that a business career offers happy escape from monotonous domestic tasks, that marriage spells drudgery in the kitchen and nothing more," the author wrote.

"It is unfair to implant in a girl's mind the thought that a business career offers happy escape from monotonous domestic tasks."

—*Good Housekeeping*, 1924

THE PITIFUL SPINSTER

"I work here," explained Ermine. "This is my job." "You work here?" Tom laughed.
"Well, you work, don't you?" she retorted, smiling. "Sure thing, but that's different."
—Dorothy Sanborn Phillips, "Wait for Me," *Good Housekeeping*, April 1924

Ermine is in love with Tom. He has graduated from college and is off to the big city to start a career as a businessman. He promises Ermine that once he is successful, he will return home to marry her. Months pass. Tom's letters arrive less frequently, and Ermy begins to fear that Tom has forgotten her. One day Ermine's friend tells her that Tom is going out at night with another woman. Everyone in town knows that Ermine has wasted her life by waiting for Tom. Poor Ermine! they whisper. She has become a spinster.

Milton is also in love—with Ermine! She doesn't know it yet though. He encourages her to take a job in her father's store. "I wasn't brought up to earn my living," Ermy tells him. "I was brought up to—" What Ermine begins to tell Milt but cannot is that she was brought up to become a wife and mother.

Ermine is, of course, a fictional character; a media image from a popular women's magazine. And yet how true is that image? According to the U.S. Census Bureau, in 1924 approximately 8.5 million women earned wages in the United States. The majority of these women were, like Ermine, single and under the age of twenty-five. Most left their jobs once they married, usually by the age of twenty-two.

But did these real-life working girls share the same thoughts as Ermine? Was their education

The media labeled a woman who was unable to entice a man to marry her a spinster—a horrible fate for any young woman who didn't heed the advice of the magazine articles and advertisements. Here a silent film depicts a lonely spinster sitting on the sidelines while a gussied-up flapper goes after a man.

and whole purpose in life to become a wife rather than an independent career woman? Yes, according to author Anna Steese Richardson. "Your daughter will probably enjoy contact in the business world," she wrote in *Good Housekeeping.* "But if she is the average normal girl . . . she knows she is merely marking time in business. Eventually she will meet the right man and marry."

That is what happens to Ermine in the story "Wait for Me." She discovers that she likes working and she's good at her job. When Tom finally returns, he is amused at her efforts to earn a living. He still wants to marry her, but Ermine realizes that Milton is the better man.

The job in the office, store, or factory was only a temporary pastime until she found "Mr. Right."

THE NEW HOUSEKEEPING AND MRS. CONSUMER

Although much of society in the 1920s believed that a woman's permanent job was to become a wife and mother, a housewife did not receive wages. And housework was indeed challenging. Earlier generations of women had labored in the home, weaving cloth, cutting and sewing clothing, molding candles, curing meats, and baking bread. In the nineteenth century, the home was a place of production. Women and young girls manufactured most of the food, clothing, and other items they needed.

By the beginning of the twentieth century, however, the American home and the housewife's tasks had undergone a change. A woman could purchase soap rather than making it at home by spending hours boiling lye and lard on a stove. She could order her clothing ready-made from a Sears®, Roebuck and Company or Montgomery Ward catalog. Rather than grow her own fresh vegetables, she could purchase canned foods. Rather than a place of production, the home had become a place of consumption.

In the 1920s, the American home continued to change—with the addition of new electric gadgets and scientific inventions for every room in the house. By 1926 approximately 80 percent of all middle- and upper-class homes had a vacuum cleaner and a washing machine. The magazine advertisements for these modern household products made bold promises. An electric washing machine reduced laundry work from five days to just one or two and eliminated rough scrubbing by hand.

A Woman's Work Is Never Done

"A man works from sun to sun, but a woman's work is never done" was once a popular saying. Women's work within the home included, among other tasks, scrubbing the bathrooms and kitchens daily, vacuuming, polishing furniture, and washing and hanging out to dry and then ironing laundry. Meal preparation required another long list of tasks, especially if a woman didn't own the latest appliances and new processed foods.

Newfangled inventions of the early decades of the 1900s promised women that their work in the home could end at sunset, if not sooner. Instead of baking bread, she could purchase from a store presliced wrapped loaves. Instead of scrambling eggs, frying bacon, and buttering toast, she might just as easily serve her family a breakfast of prepackaged cereal. Rather than boiling and stewing tomatoes and then canning in sterilized jars—a kitchen toil that took many hours, a woman could open a tin of tomatoes with a can opener and a few twists of her wrist. How much time do you spend in the kitchen? asked an advertisement for Florence oil ranges in *Good Housekeeping* in 1924. The Florence oil range cooked food more efficiently. Rather than carrying a pail of coal and shoveling it into the belly of the old-fashioned coal stoves, a women need only turn a lever and touch a match to the burner to get a flame. And the oven cooked

food more efficiently because the lever allowed the woman to control the temperature. The Florence oil range had an added benefit. Because its fuel was oil rather than coal, there were no ashes to shake down and shovel out of the stove and carry outside. Less ashy soot in the air also meant a woman's kitchen was cleaner too.

Advertisements for Hoover vacuums promised women the machine's powerful suction and special nozzle-brush could remove dirt and dust from "every conceivable resting place." Instead of beating a

One of the amazing things about this stove is that it guarantees to "save the health and the strength" of the lucky owner.

If a woman purchases this Premier Duplex vacuum cleaner, the ad claims that she will be able to enjoy her additional leisure time with a "fresher body."

rug with a broom to lift the dust, she could plug in her electric sweeper and save both time and energy. No longer did a woman have to plunge her bare arms in steaming water and hard suds to rub her laundry clean. With Rinso soap, she could soak her laundry and still achieve white and sweet-smelling cleanness.

Whether these new appliances, products, and processed foods actually saved time or created more work for women is debatable. The advertisements placed a great deal of emphasis on the importance of sanitation. The makers of Lysol, for example, told women they shouldn't just clean their bathroom sink, they had to disinfect it.

Of course, not all women suffered such drudgery. Many hired servants, called domestics, to do the household cleaning and cooking for them. Advertisements in women's magazine often showed a cheerful domestic at work in another woman's home, wearing a starched white apron and cap. She was frequently smiling. Perhaps the advertisers were suggesting her pleasure in her work was because she had been given those newfangled appliances to reduce her fatigue.

In fact, many women took work as a domestic as a last resort for earning some money to support her family. Some domestics were immigrants. Many others were African American women who found doors to other employment opportunites difficult to open. Most of these working women could not afford oil ranges or electric vacuums in their own homes. For them, a woman's work was truly never done. For when they returned home at night, there were more clothes to clean and mend, floors to sweep, and meals to prepare. Long hours and low wages convinced many to give up their aprons and caps for other work . . . if they could find it.

THE EDUCATION OF LILLIAN GILBRETH

When her husband Frank died in 1924, Lillian Gilbreth became a single working mother. She continued her own studies and professional work while encouraging her children to follow educational and career aspirations of their own. All of Lillian and Frank Gilbreth's children graduated from college and lived long and healthy lives, as did Lillian herself.

When Lillian Moller married Frank Gilbreth in 1904, the wedding announcement in her local newspaper included this line: "Although a graduate of the University of California, the bride is nonetheless an extremely attractive young woman." Lillian Gilbreth was a psychologist, but she was also a wife and mother of many children—eventually twelve! If the newspaper editors viewed her college degree with suspicion, they must have been truly surprised when this industrious mother earned her doctorate degree in 1915.

At the turn of the century, many people, including doctors, believed that education was too stressful for women. Their bodies were not strong enough to endure long hours of intense study. Some even went so far as to suggest that women might contract tuberculosis if they taxed their bodies with too much textbook knowledge. In fact, Gilbreth became ill with pleurisy, another form of lung disease, while studying for her master's degree. Fortunately, she paid no attention to those who implied that the disease was a result of her studies. She soon recovered and returned to school.

Electric stoves and furnaces meant no more layers of coal soot over the surfaces of the house, cutting the amount of the time necessary to clean. Electric lights were not only brighter but safer than gas fixtures, which could emit dangerous fumes. Even the telephone could be a modern tool of housekeeping. It cut the time necessary for a woman to walk or drive to a store for purchasing foodstuffs or clothing. It could also be a kitchen convenience, according to an advertisement text for the Bell Telephone Company. The ad stated that "in smaller homes, the kitchen telephone is especially important . . . in avoiding, for instance, such domestic tragedies as burnt biscuits or scorched roasts."

"Domestic tragedies" apparently happened frequently before the introduction of these wonderful scientific inventions. In a cookbook, the makers of Hotpoint electric ranges explained the old way of determining the temperature of a coal-fired oven: "The *experienced* housewife put her hand in the oven and 'judged' the heat and thereby served delicious cakes and pies; but the *inexperienced* housewife, without 'cooking sense,' served failures." Switch to an electric stove, however, and failures disappear: "When you know the temperature for baking a cake all anxiety . . . is needless!" Moreover, the author of the cookbook adds, "The one

who cooks electrically saves time, money and strength."

Christine Frederick was the housekeeping editor of *Ladies' Home Journal.* She called the modern housewife's work "the new housekeeping" and the modern housewife "Mrs. Consumer." Mrs. Consumer was an educated woman not easily fooled by

Christine Frederick (right) *is shown in about 1930 conducting one of her many domestically oriented scientific experiments.*

false advertising or untrue claims for a product's effectiveness, she said. How Mrs. Consumer spent her time at her "permanent job" was the subject of Christine Frederick's magazine articles.

Bring science into the home, she urged Mrs. Consumer. The result would be less fatigue, and that meant more time to enjoy family or leisure activities. Purchasing the latest appliances was just one way to bring science into the home. Applying principles of organization and time-saving motion to the tasks of cleaning a home could also make the housewife's job easier.

In one column, Christine Frederick explained that it took her forty-five minutes each night to scrape, wash, and dry the dinner dishes, including forty-eight pieces of china, twenty-two pieces of silver, and ten utensils and pots—eighty pieces in all! "Like all other women I thought that there couldn't be much improvement in the same old task of washing dishes," she wrote. But Christine Frederick found a way.

In a factory, she explained, the necessary tools were right next to the worker and at the proper level so as to eliminate bending, reaching, or walking away from the workstation. This saved time and the worker's energy so the worker could accomplish more. Christine Frederick recommended that housewives organize their homes, especially their kitchens, in much the same way as factories were organized. Place knives and cooking products near the work surface. In her own home, Frederick raised the level of the washbasin to avoid bending over as she washed dishes. She scraped all the dishes at one time, stacking them on her right side. She moved her drainboard to the left side and saved a few

"Like all other women I thought that there couldn't be much improvement in the same old task of washing dishes."

—Christine Frederick, 1912

seconds for each dish by not having to switch from one hand to the other, and she washed, then rinsed. Finally, she poured scalding water on the dishes and let them dry without wiping while she worked on the pots and pans. In all, she reduced her task of washing the dinner dishes by fifteen minutes!

Fifteen minutes a day may not seem like much. But multiplied by seven days a week, fifty-two weeks a year—why, the savings amounted to more than one week away from the kitchen sink!

Frederick wrote about a young bride proudly showing off her new kitchen to her. "Isn't it a beauty?" the bride beamed. Frederick saw what the bride did not: The kitchen had all the modern appliances, but the room itself was poorly organized. "Her stove was in a recess of the kitchen at one end and her pantry was twenty feet [6 m] away at the opposite end," Frederick wrote. "Every time she wanted to use a frying-pan she had to walk twenty feet to get it, and after using it she had to walk twenty feet to put it away."

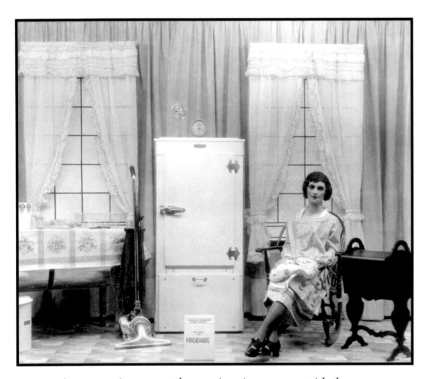

A mannequin portrays the new American woman with the very latest machines: an electric vacuum and a Frigidaire. With such incredible conveniences, it is no wonder that the manufacturers place the woman at leisure in her kitchen, working on embroidery.

Lillian Gilbreth was a working woman, a housewife, and a mother of twelve children. Like Christine Frederick, she encouraged women to think of their homes as workplaces and to plan space and time efficiently. She designed modern kitchens so that the sink and stove were at the best possible height to prevent unnecessary strain. The goal, she said, was not to bake more pies in a day but rather to bake the pies faster and so have time to devote to the children. She called this work simplification.

Other popular women's magazines of the 1920s also offered tips on how to complete household tasks more easily and in less time. The goal of these articles was both to educate the young housewife and to instill in her a sense of pride in a job well done. In "The Way We Clean Windows," the editor of *Good Housekeeping* emphasized the pride that could come from caring for one's home. "In spite of the fact that we all consider window cleaning a bugbear," she wrote, "I doubt if there is one of us who, after completing the task, does not feel a sense of . . . pride and enjoyment at seeing the windows sparkle."

The hard work of keeping a house clean had its rewards, the magazines told its readers. In the 1920s, being a good wife and mother meant sparkling windows, clean dishes and laundry, and vacuumed rugs. Good housekeeping was a virtue, an expression of a woman's love for her family. Of course, the flip side to that coin was this: if a woman was not a good housekeeper—if her windows were grimy, her sheets more gray than white—then perhaps she didn't care for her family as much as she should. The media's image of the "perfect" wife and mother could have harmful implications for women.

SCIENTIFIC MOTHERHOOD

Whereas earlier generations of women had believed in a mother's instinct in caring for her children, the science-smart media of the 1920s told modern women otherwise. Intuition and instinct simply weren't enough. Nor was the advice of family and friends who had raised children themselves. Instead, a mother needed knowledge of scientific methods to raise healthy and socially responsible children.

Exactly what scientific knowledge did young mothers need? First, they should understand what and when to feed a baby. But mothers have

Miss Anne Raymond took her radio assignment of offering scientific nutrition advice under the title of the health fairy quite seriously. She is shown broadcasting in costume over the radiophone from the General Electric station WGY at Schenectady, New York, in 1922.

always needed to know that. The difference in the 1920s was a focus on modern-day formulas and the need to keep an infant on a strict daily schedule. Scientific motherhood also required knowing which vitamins, proteins, and carbohydrates a child needed to grow strong. It meant involving the child in proper exercises to strengthen muscles. It required the safe preparation of food and the avoidance of germs and disease. Women who lacked this scientific information risked harming their children permanently. At least, that is what articles published in newspapers, magazines, and advice books suggested.

A newspaper called the *Odyssey* praised scientific motherhood, stating that experts could help a young mother bring up her child properly. The paper claimed that most young mothers simply didn't know what was best for their child until they had three or four babies. Then, through sheer trial and error, they had figured it all out. But that was the old-fashioned way.

Advertisers jumped on the scientific motherhood bandwagon. They created advertisements that emphasized science—or at least *sounded* scientific. Imperial Granum Food for babies, for example, compared feeding a baby to building a house. The text stated that "the secret of a finely built house" was its well-constructed foundation. To build a "foundation of good health" in an infant was a mother's first responsibility, and Imperial Granum Food was the answer. The advertisement instructed mothers that if they mixed Imperial Granum Food with cow's milk, they could avoid the formation of "hard curds" in the baby's stomach. Quite likely, most young mothers did not know what a hard curd was or why it formed from drinking cow's milk. The text was an advertisement, written not by a doctor but a copywriter. No matter. In an age of "experts know best," most young mothers welcomed the advice.

Child-rearing columnist Myrtle Meyer Eldred was herself a mother, but she held no medical or science degree. Nevertheless, women across the country hungered for her child-rearing advice. Myrtle Meyer's column, *Your Baby and Mine*, appeared once a week in newspapers across the country. Mothers wrote to her for advice, most often about feeding. And most often, Eldred's response was rooted in the popular "science" of the day. She wrote to one mother:

> *Thirty-six ounces of milk is too much for any baby. One quart daily is sufficient. You are . . . entirely forgetting that he should be having both cereal and vegetables as well as orange juice at eight months of age. Fine wheat cereals, well cooked, can be given at the*

10 o'clock and 6 o'clock feedings, starting with teaspoonful amounts and increasing cautiously until the baby can take one to three table-spoons at a feeding. Give orange juice or tomato juice one-half to one hour before morning feeding. Put one uncooked egg yolk in the 2 o'clock feeding and give a tablespoon or so of finely sieved carrot or spinach. In this way you get in all the elements necessary to the child's diet.

The instructions were complicated. Modern historians who read Eldred's columns wonder at her lack of understanding that not all babies are alike. Not all children require the same amount of food. And they don't all eat at the same time. But in Eldred's scientific eyes, babies weren't individuals. They were more like little machines that a mother-mechanic could adjust and fix so that they operated properly.

There was no end to advice on scientific motherhood in the popular media. Even tickling took on a scientific purpose. "Tickling is splendid for a baby," *Time* magazine reported in 1925, quoting Sir Harry E. Bruce-Porter, a London specialist in children's diseases. It "makes babies laugh and thus develops their lungs."

In *Hygeia*, a public health magazine

Good Housekeeping

OCTOBER 1929

25 CENTS
15 CENTS IN CANADA

CASTLES IN SPAIN *By Frances Parkinson Keyes*
Mariel Brady ~ Frederic F. Van de Water ~ Sarah Addington
Emma-Lindsay Squier ~ Konrad Bercovici
PARIS AUTUMN OPENINGS

The covers of women's magazines of the 1920s and 1930s featured sweet mother-enjoying-child scenes. But the inside editorial content offered regimented instructions for new mothers, who were told that they needed the benefit of science in order to raise children properly.

published by the American Medical Association, author Jessie Fenton explained how a mother can teach her baby safety. She wrote:

The first lesson may be to give up things he has hold of which may hurt him. Safety pins are conven-ient for the first lessons. Every time the mother changes the baby's dia-pers, she can take time to place one of the pins in the child's hand for a moment. Then she can say to him, "Give it to me," at the same time taking it away again. Then she should praise him in a gay and lively manner and romp with him a little, so that he will have a pleasant association with the game and will feel that he has done something that is fun.

Teaching a child how not to fall—something children do all the time—involved a simple but specific set of directions. According to *Hygeia:* Place the baby tummy-side down on a bed. Slide him gently backward until his legs hang over the edge. Continue to draw him down until his feet touch the floor. Allow the child to creep away. By following this procedure, said the author, the baby would soon learn the proper way to climb down from a high place.

This emphasis on scientific motherhood suggested that women in the 1920s were not just wives and mothers. They were professional women whose job was tremendously important. "You are building your baby's future now!" read the advertising text for Imperial Granum baby food. What could be more important than that?

Despite women's interest in the latest scientific knowledge about running a house and caring for a baby, not all women followed the advice of the experts. Thousands of women didn't bother to switch their drainboard from the right side of the sink to save time while washing dishes. Many thousands more did not feed their babies by the hands on a clock or the number of ounces in a bottle.

Housewives and mothers were not "docile sheep," Christine Frederick told the leaders of the business world. These leaders were mostly men who manufactured the new housekeeping gadgets. Don't ignore the opinions of Mrs. Consumer, Christine Frederick warned. Those businessmen who did would risk a loss of profits or even bankruptcy. Men might earn the money, but Mrs. Consumer spent it. Advertisers in particular listened and learned.

Ads of the 1920s seemed to have an almost alarmist tone—pointing out the consequences if one did not use the advertiser's product. A woman without the correct beauty products would be pitied by society (left). But an even worse fate was in store for the woman with bad breath—spinsterhood (right)!

THE POWER OF SUGGESTION . . . AND DECEPTION

In the 1920s, mass advertising was born. Popular magazines and daily newspapers were a terrific way for advertisers to reach millions of readers—especially women. In an attempt to sell their products, advertisers preyed on three emotions: vanity, shame, and fear.

You've got to give people a "reason why" to buy a product, said advertising executive Albert Lasker. Helen Woodward was also a prominent advertising executive during the 1920s, one of the few women to rise to such a position of power in the business. Her approach was to tell women the dangers that would ensue if they didn't buy a product. People will gossip about you. Your children may become ill. Your husband may lose interest in you. All these claims were woven subtly into advertising texts, often through short narratives, or stories.

Advertising narratives had characters and conflicts. Even a single photograph or illustration on a magazine cover suggested "story" and meaning. The major character was most often a woman, with minor roles played by husbands, children, and spying, gossiping neighbors. "Low voices . . . meaning nods . . . well-bred eyes observing more than they are willing to betray . . . what a silent drama of admiration or disapproval is played when you have left the room," read the opening lines of an advertisement for Devoe Paint and Varnish. "Betrayed!" was the title of an advertisement for Listerine. It began: "At a distance she had appeared unusually neat, immaculate. But upon their first face-to-face meeting he discovered that her teeth were not clean."

The women in these advertisements were most often pictured as middle- or upper-class and white. Women of color rarely appeared in advertisements, and when they did, they were in the role of servants. Poor women were invisible, unseen among the pages of the magazines, though they, too, cleaned their homes and prepared meals. But the middle- and upper-class woman was the Mrs. Consumer the advertisers most wanted to persuade to purchase their products. "Sally," for example, is a character in an advertising narrative for Rogers Brother Silverware. She is the perfect wife, the helpmate for her husband as he builds his career. The text mentions nothing about Sally's needs, only her husband's. The house isn't "theirs." It is "his":

> *What a wife Sally is! No wonder they call a fellow's wife his "better half"! Just look at the way Sally had helped him all the way along. Somehow, through her, just the people he*

Poor women were invisible, unseen among the pages of the magazines, though they, too, cleaned their homes and prepared meals.

needed to know, he always did know. Just the impression he wanted his home to make, it always did make—because of Sally. And now, with the members of his firm and their wives invited for dinner tonight, the table is perfectly appointed, even to the last salad fork and orange spoon. Sally again!

The images of women were often conflicting. On the cover of the April 1922 *Ladies' Home Journal*, a knight on a white horse carries away a lovely maiden. On the back cover, however, is a full-page advertisement for Old Dutch Cleanser. The woman is on her knees scrubbing her bathroom. Are love and marriage as romantic as the image of the maid in the knight's arms? Or is marriage

A woman looking at a magazine of the 1920s had to ask herself which she was—the elegant woman in satin on the front cover or the woman in an apron cleaning her sink on the back cover? Perhaps she was expected to be both?

nothing more than the drudgery of serving a husband and keeping his "castle" clean?

Two words that appear frequently in women's magazine advertisements of the early 1920s are *drudgery* and *dainty*. Housework was drudgery. Housewives were dainty. The concept seems like a contradiction. One doesn't ordinary think of dainty, delicate creatures doing grinding and boring work. These examples come from advertisements published in women's magazines in the 1920s:

> *Three meals a day, 366 days this year; the ordering, the cooking and then the monotonous round of dishes. What a difference bright, cheerful surroundings make to you. . . . And how simple it is to make household tasks pleasanter and easier.*
> —ad for Nairn linoleum

> *Women with soft, dainty hands . . . now launder their own precious stockings and blouses . . . in gentle Ivory suds which is as harmless to hands as it is to the dainty garments themselves.*
> —ad for Ivory Soap Flakes

Advertisements like these paint a picture of the American woman in the 1920s. But the picture is not always accurate. Advertisers were using the narratives and visual images to appeal to people's emotions.

Fleischmann's is a manufacturer of yeast products. Yeast is a group of fungi. As an ingredient in bread, it helps to make the dough rise. For years, Fleischmann's has been selling yeast (in the form of small square cakes, or packets) to housewives who baked bread in the home. With the coming of modern times, however, the average consumer purchased more of her baked goods and thus baked less. Fleischmann's sales began to drop. They needed a new reason for people to purchase their product. They found it with the help of an advertising agency called the J. Walter Thompson Company.

Judging by the advertisements of the 1920s, the modern woman was no longer delicate. She liked to have fun, enjoyed the company of men, and believed that science could solve most of her household problems. Nevertheless, whether the modern woman was a career woman, wife, or mother, she had lots of problems. Her breath was bad, and her gums bled. She had body odor and athlete's foot. She was constipated. Her skin was dull and wrinkled. While both men and women of all social classes experience some of these bodily problems, the advertisers most often targeted middle- and upper-class white women. Their appeal, or selling strategy, was shame or embarrassment for her imperfect body.

This line from an advertisement for Absorbine Jr. foot treatment plays on a woman's vanity and fear of offending: "His heart quickened at the soft fragrance of her cheeks but her shoes hid a sorry case of athlete's foot."

"Intestinal fatigue" was a euphemism (or less offensive word) for constipation. The solution was a yeast cake developed by Fleischmann's. Rather than using the vulgar "armpit," the advertisers for Odorono suggested the location of body odor by saying "within the curve of a woman's arm."

Bad breath was a vulgar term to apply to the exhalations of middle- and upper-class women—*Halitosis* sounded more scientific. In the 1920s, advertisers often suggested that scientific solutions, such as germ-killing Listerine, could solve the problem. The definition of halitosis is in parenthesis, as if being whispered.

The thing was troubling her—something she had overheard several men say about her when they thought she was the last person in the world within hearing distance. . . . That's the insidious thing about halitosis (unpleasant breath). You, yourself, rarely know when you have it. And even your closest friends won't tell you.

Advertisers of the 1920s often proposed new uses for their products. Yeast was offered for constipation, and Listerine had a short-lived ad campaign as a douche.

"*Bad Skin* is usually Nature punishing you for internal neglect—"

THE DOCTOR who makes the above statement is one of the most famous skin specialists in Italy, Dr. Pietro Bosellini, Professor of Dermatology in the great University of Rome.

Dr. Bosellini states:—

"Skin troubles as a rule must be attacked from *inside* the body. When waste matter collects and stagnates in the body, the blood absorbs poisons. The resistance of the skin to infection is weakened and . . . pimples, boils or blotches may then appear."

To correct this condition, Dr. Bosellini advises, not drugs or medicines, but . . . *yeast!*

"Fresh yeast (he says) has remarkable power to . . . restore regular evacuations. The effect on the health is often remarkable. Digestion improves; headaches cease; *skin troubles soon clear up.*"

At any grocery, and most restaurants and soda fountains, you can get *Fleischmann's Yeast*. Just eat it daily — 3 cakes a day — before meals, or between meals and at bedtime — plain, or dissolved in water (about a third of a glass).

Then notice, after say 30 to 60 days, how much clearer your complexion has become.

Fleischmann's Yeast, you know, *stimulates* the intestines . . . softens the waste in the body so you can eliminate it easily. The result is, your system is "toned." The poisons that were causing your bad skin, bad breath, headaches, indigestion and general "run-down" feeling are cleared away.

Fleischmann's Yeast, also, is very rich, you know, in health-giving vitamins B, G and D. Why not try eating it regularly — starting today?

"*Our faces were so broken out, we dreaded to appear in public*"

"My sister and I both had skin trouble," writes Miss Virginia Koons (at left in photo) of *Miami Beach, Fla.* "We were so embarrassed we dreaded appearing in public. To add to our troubles, boils appeared . . . A doctor had advised yeast for one of our friends . . . We tried it, and in a week noticed improvement. Fleischmann's Yeast entirely cleared up our skin troubles."

declares
DR. PIETRO BOSELLINI
of Rome

Important

Fleischmann's Yeast for health comes only in the foil-wrapped cake with the yellow label. The yeast in fresh, effective form—the kind doctors advise. Write for booklet. Standard Brands Inc.—Dept. Y-A-5, 691 Washington St., N. Y. C.

Copyright 1932, Standard Brands Incorporated

Advertisers of the 1920s slanted their ads in whatever direction would produce the most sales. When Fleischmann's sales as a baking aid dropped, the product was pushed as a source of vitamins, then a cure for constipation. In the ad above, Fleischmann's is said to be the path to a good complexion.

In a full-page advertisement, they featured testimony from a German physician as well as a young mother. The physician stated that yeast helped to cleanse the intestines and that, in turn, cured many skin blemishes such as acne and boils. The physician recommended that people eat three Fleischmann's cakes each day. The same advertisement showed a photograph of a young mother with two healthy children. Her testimony was personal but equally persuasive:

> "*I was old before my time,*" writes Mrs. Mabel Kinneer of Staten Island, New York. "*As long as I can remember I had suffered from constipation. As I grew worse and worse, I visited a stomach specialist. He recommended three cakes a day of Fleischmann's Yeast. Half-heartedly, I began. But very soon I noticed improvement. Now I am well.*"

Both testimonies were misleading. Eating yeast did not cure skin problems, as the German doctor claimed. The advertising agency, however, had paid the doctor hundreds of dollars to make the statement. Kinneer had also accepted money for her statement. Furthermore, a government investigation into the Fleischmann's "Yeast for Health" campaign revealed that Kinneer was not quite the person she appeared to be in the advertisement.

The investigation of the U.S. Federal Trade Commission revealed that the people featured in the advertisements were from the lower classes had dressed them in clothing that suggested they were people of wealth or social prominence. They photographed these people in locations that suggested wealth and social standing. The advertising agency had photographed Kinneer and her two children first at a polo ground in a wealthy Long Island neighborhood and later at a ferry landing in New Jersey.

The Fleischmann's advertisement appeared in women's magazines, including *Ladies' Home Journal.* Although it influenced consumers and temporarily helped yeast sales, it was an attempt to deceive the consumer.

THE PROBLEM WITH AUNT JEMIMA

Nancy Green was born a slave in Kentucky in 1834. Despite her impoverished beginnings, however, she would become one of the most famous women in the United States. No one knew her real name. They knew her only by her red bandanna and wide, white-toothed smile. Nancy Green was the first woman to portray Aunt Jemima.

As a free woman, Nancy Green had moved from Kentucky to Chicago, where she found work in the home of Judge Walker. She was both a cook and a nanny for the judge's two sons. Nancy Green was a wonderful cook, and she had an outgoing and cheerful personality. Her reputation brought her to the attention of one of the judge's friends. He knew of a manufacturing company that was searching for a black woman who might represent their new product, a self-rising pancake mix. The R. T. Davis Mill Company had already decided to use the name Aunt Jemima, an idea they got from song in a minstrel show—a variety show in which white people performed in blackface makeup. They had both a product and a name. All they needed was an image.

THE BLACK MAMMY MONUMENT

In 1923, the same year that Nancy Green died, the United Daughters of the Confederacy lobbied to build a new historical monument in Washington, D.C. The Daughters' goal was to promote Confederate (Southern) heritage. But the women didn't suggest a monument to plantations or southern farmers. Instead, they proposed to honor black mammies—the slave women who cared for the plantation owner's children rather than working in the fields. To raise money, the organization printed fund-raising literature. In one publication, the organizers asked, "Did you not have an 'Old Black Mammy' who loved and cared for you in the days of your youth whose memory and spirit you want perpetuated?'" The old black mammy was part of the Old South. The monument would honor her.

African American communities were infuriated. Yes, black mammies were part of the Old South. Black mammies, however, were enslaved. They were not, as racial stereotypes suggested, smiling, contented, and loyal to their masters. Their protests, in part, defeated the proposal.

African Americans would rail against racial stereotypes of the black mammy in other cultural images, including films of the 1920s and 1930s. They also objected to advertisements for such products as Aunt Jemima pancake mix.

In suggesting a monument to the black mammy, the members of the United Daughters of the Confederacy felt they were honoring the women who had played such an important part in their upbringing. But the black community of the early 1920s did not appreciate a monument that commemorated slavery.

Nancy Green signed a contract with the Davis Company to portray the fictional Aunt Jemima. She was fifty-nine years old. Her first public appearance was in 1893 at the Chicago World's Exposition. She served millions of pancakes there. She also sang and told stories. So popular was her exhibit that police were needed to keep the crowds moving in an orderly way. The Nancy Green success story continued long after the world's fair ended. She traveled across the country with her pancakes, songs, and stories. Sales of Aunt Jemima pancake mix soared.

When Nancy Green died in 1923, the makers of the pancake mix did not at first look for a new representative. By this time, the Davis Company had sold its product to the Quaker Oats Company. In 1933 the advertising team for Quaker Oats discovered Anna Robinson. She was a big woman, weighing 350 pounds (160 kilograms). Like Nancy Green, she appeared at exhibits nationwide. She posed with movie stars for publicity purposes. The company hired an artist to paint her portrait. It later appeared smiling from the millions of boxes of pancake mix in stores across the country. The company also created phony legends for their fictional character. One claimed that during the Civil War (1861–1865), the original Aunt Jemima had helped a Confederate colonel to escape by serving the Union (Northern) soldiers a heaping batch of her steaming pancakes.

To encourage further sales, the company produced product premiums. In 1918 mothers could send a nickel plus a box top to the Quaker Oats Company to receive the pattern and material to sew an Aunt Jemima doll for their little girls. The doll was fat with heavy red lips and dressed in an apron.

Clearly, Aunt Jemima pancake mix was a popular product. The secret to its success was the use of powdered milk so that all the housewife had to do was add water and stir. It was likely the first convenience food of the twentieth century. The product's success was also due to the advertising strategy that used real-life women to represent the fictional Aunt Jemima.

Clearly, Aunt Jemima pancake mix was a popular product. The secret to its success was the use of powdered milk so that all the housewife had to do was add water and stir.

Why did advertisers choose a black woman? Why did they cover her head in a red bandanna and portray her as a smiling, contented "mammy," reminiscent of plantation life during the slavery era? The answer lives not just in advertising planning but also in cultural stereotypes. The red bandanna was more than just a head dressing. It was a symbol of domestic service. A black woman in a red bandanna suggested slavery. Likewise, the myth of a black mammy saving a Confederate officer from Union soldiers smacked of racial bias. The rag doll pattern with its oversized red lips was a racial stereotype as well.

A survey conducted in 1920 in two southern cities—Nashville, Tennessee, and Richmond, Virginia—confirmed the negative connotations that the image had among African Americans. The survey presented two images for the pancake mix. In one, Aunt Jemima was the dominant element. In the other, the pancakes dominated the image. Overwhelmingly, African Americans denounced the first image. The image suggested slavery, they said. The use of a log cabin and the head rag suggested African American women were illiterate mammies.

Aunt Jemima's image on the package of pancake mix was just one way of advertising the product. Quaker Oats also ran print advertisements in popular women's magazines. In a 1918 issue of *Ladies' Home Journal*, Aunt Jemima speaks to the reader using a southern dialect but one that suggests she is, in fact, uneducated.

Advertisers create images to sell a product. And yet advertising images serve other purposes. The images influence our perceptions of others and even ourselves, sometimes positively and sometimes negatively. In the case of Aunt Jemima, an advertising success story for a worthy product promoted a negative racial stereotype that would continue for decades.

Chapter Three
Morals and Manners

"What's the matter with girls today?" Dad kept asking. "Don't they know what those greasy-haired boys are after? Don't they know what's going to happen to them if they go around showing their legs through silk stockings, and with bare knees, and with skirts so short that the slightest wind doesn't leave anything to the imagination?"

"Well, that's the way everybody dresses today," Anne insisted. "Everybody but Ernestine and me; we're school freaks. Boys don't notice things like that when everybody dresses that way."

—Frank B. Gilbreth Jr. and Ernestine Gilbreth Carey,
reflecting on their 1920s childhood in the novel *Cheaper by the Dozen*, 1948

In his 1931 book, *Only Yesterday,*

Frederick Lewis Allen describes the old moral code that ruled American families before the Great War. Men were the breadwinners who supported the family's needs of food, clothing, and shelter. Women were the moral guardians of the home. From them, youth learned right from wrong. Right from wrong included a long list of dos and don'ts, especially for good girls.

Good girls wore corsets instead of that newfangled invention, the brassiere. They did not wear silk stockings, satiny lingerie called teddies, bathing suits that revealed their legs, or high-heeled shoes. Rouge, lipstick, mascara, and perfume—none of these artificial paints and fragrances had a place on her dresser top.

Good girls were never tempted to do bad things, such as smoking cigarettes or drinking alcohol. In some states, a woman could be arrested for smoking in public. And in all states, beginning in 1920, when Congress passed the Eighteenth Amendment, the manufacture, sale, and transportation of alcohol was against the law. But people still purchased bootleg, or illegal, liquor during Prohibition (1920–1933). Even so, good girls never indulged in drinking liquor or showed signs of intoxication.

Good girls longed for romantic love and happily-ever-after lives. They pursued their future husbands through cat-and-mouse games in which the good girl appeared to be innocent, helpless, and in need of rescuing.

By the 1920s, however, the idea of what was right and wrong began to change. The length of skirts rose inches from the ground. Young girls discarded their corsets, saying that boys did not want to dance with girls who wore them. Even in well-to-do and respected families, good girls were defiantly

Prohibition did not seem to phase the free-thinking women of the 1920s. Despite the fact that the manufacture and sale of liquor was illegal at the time, this woman happily displays her specially designed flask-concealing boot for the camera. Facing page: Flaunting her smoking with a fancy cigarette holder was part of the flapper's fashionable image.

smoking cigarettes in public where anybody could see. "There were stories of daughters of the most exemplary parents getting drunk 'blotto' as their companions cheerfully put it," wrote Frederick Lewis Allen. "And worst of all, even at well-regulated dances they were said to retire where the eye of the most sharp-sighted chaperone could not follow, and in darkened rooms or in parked cars to engage in the unspeakable practice of petting and necking."

The good girls and boys who had been children during the Great War had become teenagers and young adults. They were "making mincemeat" of the old moral code, said Allen. A popular song from 1921 captured the spirit of youth:

> *In the morning, in the evening,*
> *Ain't we got fun?*
> *Not much money, oh but honey,*
> *Ain't we got fun?*

The age of the flapper had arrived.

The Flapper Rebellion

A flapper was a young woman, usually between the ages of fifteen and twenty-five. While not every modern girl in the 1920s was a flapper, every flapper shared similar characteristics. First, her clothing defined her. Her dress was often low cut, revealing neck and throat and sometimes more. The skirt rose to just an inch (2.5 centimeters) below her knees. She wore silk stockings, the tops of which she rolled and twisted, to just below the knee.

Flappers were the epitome of modern. In addition to the cloche hat and shapeless shift, among the musts for the fashionable flapper were short, sleek hair; a flat chest; and face makeup (more than likely applied in public).

Music Madness

A 1926 Life *magazine cover depicts the rigors of the latest dance craze—the Charleston. Medical authorities worried that such an active dance might be too rigorous for delicate young women.*

Music teacher Anne Shaw Faulkner blamed popular music for corrupting modern girls. She herself favored the waltzes and two-steps that had been so popular in the years before the Great War. That music, with its regular rhythm, melody, and harmony, soothed the nerves. Flappers, however, preferred jazz music with its blaring brass horns and syncopated, or irregular, beat. The only way to move to such jerky music was to swing your arms, kick your legs, and shake your shoulders and hips. She believed that jazz could twist the dancer's spine out of alignment and that the off-key tones and jerky rhythm had a harmful effect on listeners. She even said that jazz confused a person's sense of right and wrong. Faulkner claimed that scientists had proven this theory in a study of jazz music and mentally ill patients. Who were the scientists? What was the study? Faulkner never said.

The Charleston remained popular for most of the decade. Two flappers who traveled to Germany for a summer vacation began dancing the Charleston in a Salzburg, Austria, hotel. According to news reports, the astonished band stopped playing and a shocked hotel manager ushered the flappers out of the room. The next song the band played was the "Blue Danube Waltz."

The Charleston posed more than a health or a moral threat to society, however. In 1925 the chief of police in Passaic, New Jersey, banned the Charleston from dance halls. He did so, he told reporters, not because he thought the dance was immoral. Instead, he feared the construction of the dance halls could not support the wild stomping movements of the dancers and might, in fact, collapse!

Her dress was shapeless, more like a sack without a waist. And it was skimpy and lightweight. Whereas the dresses of an earlier generation had required as much as 20 yards (18 m) of fabric, the flapper's dress took 7 yards (6 m). When a breeze wafted by, the skirt lifted, revealing the flapper's bare knees.

The pastor of Calvary Baptist Church in New York gave a sermon on the immodest clothing of the flapper. He recited a poem from the pulpit:

> *Mary had a little skirt,*
> *The latest style, no doubt,*
> *But every time she got inside,*
> *She was more than half way out!*

Underneath "Mary's little skirt," she wore a step-in, a single piece of lingerie that took the place of the stiff-boned corset. The step-in allowed her to move freely—which was a good thing when dancing the Charleston. Such loose-fitting clothes symbolized the flapper's lifestyle. She would not be bound by the old rules or even the old music.

Hair also defined the flapper. The bob was a short haircut, shingled very close to the neck. Like the clothing flappers wore, bobbed hair was also revealing. It showed the flesh on the back of the flapper's neck and even her ears! (Women in previous centuries had avoided showing too much skin.) Bruce Bliven, editor for the *New Republic* magazine, called the flapper's costume, including her bobbed hair, "The New Nakedness."

Why did women dress this way? Bliven asked. In an article he wrote in 1925 titled "Flapper Jane," he imagined the flapper's answer: "In a

Movie actress Louise Brooks is sporting what was known as the soft bob of the early 1920s. It was an earlier version of the more severe cut known as the Eton crop, which came into vogue in the mid-1920s. By then, the stylish woman was wearing her hair much shorter and slicked against her head.

way," says Jane, "it's just honesty. Women have come down off the pedestal lately. They are tired of this mysterious-feminine-charm stuff.

"Women still want to be loved," explains Jane . . . but for who they really were and not for some ideal image of womanhood. Not all women were ready right off the bat for marriage or in the language of the flapper, for the "home-and-baby act." A bachelor girl should be able to do what a bachelor man does — 50-50, equal split.

"Women still want to be loved," explains Jane . . . but for who they really were and not for some ideal image of womanhood. Not all women were ready right off the bat for marriage or in the language of the flapper, for the "home-and-baby act."

—Bruce Bliven, "Flapper Jane," 1925

Some people in society blamed the war for triggering this rebellion of youth. They claimed it had upset the balance of the sexes and, in particular, confused women about their role in society and where they truly belonged—in the workplace or at home. During the war, women had assumed the jobs of men who had become soldiers. Once women tasted independence, both mentally and economically, they didn't want to go back to being hidden inside a house, even if it did have all the latest modern appliances.

Others blamed the flappers' rebellion on the Nineteenth Amendment. Giving women the right to vote put ideas in their heads, these people argued. It made women think they should be equal in all facets of life—not just in the voting booth.

Flappers did believe in equality. And yet they were not necessarily feminists who marched with picket signs in front of polling booths or unfair workplaces. In fact, the flappers' rebellion was all about having fun in social situations. Few flappers cared who ran the country or the factories.

One element that contributed to the flappers' rebellion was the amazing increase in the number of automobiles in the United States. Before the war, cars were purchased mostly by wealthy families for recreation. But Henry Ford's decision to use mass production in his factories brought the price of cars down to a level more people could afford. By the 1920s, the automobile was no longer the "rich man's toy." It was the common man's—and woman's—symbol of progress, excitement, and freedom.

Gentlemen Prefer Blondes—but Marry Brunettes

Her name was Lorelei Lee. She was blonde and single, not very smart in a book-learning way but very ambitious. She didn't long for a career. Her heart's desires were fixed on furs. Diamond bracelets were her best friends. The best way to acquire these expensive fashion accessories was to acquire a wealthy husband. Finding the right man was not a matter of love. Love was abstract. A girl couldn't wrap love around her shoulders the way she could a fur stole. Love did not glitter in the sunlight like a diamond necklace. No, for Lorelei, love wasn't important, but a man's income—and willingness to spend a good amount of it on her—was.

Although best remembered for her novel, Anita Loos (above) *was a successful screenplay writer. She went from writing subtitles for silent movies to scripting screenplays for such classics as* Red-Headed Woman (1932) *and* San Francisco (1936).

Lorelei Lee made her first social appearance in the pages of *Harper's Bazaar.* She was a fictional character in a series of stories created by author Anita Loos. In 1926 Loos published her stories about Lorelei in a novel titled *Gentlemen Prefer Blondes.* The book and its blonde heroine became an international sensation. The best seller was soon made into a Broadway play and later into a Hollywood movie starring Marilyn Monroe as Lorelei.

Loos got the idea for Lorelei's character while traveling by train with a friend. Anita Loos was brunette. Her friend was blonde. Gentlemen on the train were far more attentive to Anita Loos's friend than to her. Mile after mile, as the train crossed the Midwest, Loos observed her friend's power over men. Men stepped aside for the blonde, but not the brunette. When her friend dropped a magazine, men leaped to fetch it. Loos was certain she herself was every bit as attractive as her blonde girlfriend. She knew she was a good deal smarter. The attraction, Loos concluded, was the color of her friend's hair! As the train rocked along, Loos picked up her pen and began to write.

In creating Lorelei Lee, Anita Loos created a social stereotype—or at least tapped into an existing stereotype. Lorelei is a gold digger, a label society uses to describe a woman whose ambitions are to wheedle expensive things from men. In the novel, Lorelei's best friend is Dorothy. Like Loos, Dorothy is brunette and a good deal smarter and more practical than Lorelei. The novel's satirical portrayal of men and women's relationships, as told through Lorelei's diary entries, made *Gentlemen Prefer Blondes* a media sensation. Critics loved it.

The car gave women freedom to go wherever they wished and without a chaperone. Even Emily Post agreed in her popular book of etiquette published in 1922 that it was socially acceptable for a young woman to motor alone. And automobiles created other opportunities only dreamed of before. Young men and young women could escape their parents' parlors and go for a drive. The privacy of a car parked along a shady lane meant they could snuggle and even kiss.

"It's terribly exciting," one girl said about this new trend in dating. "I think it is natural to want nice men to kiss you, so why not do what is natural?"

Silent movies were another element thought to fire the flappers' wild spirits. Movies provided darkened surroundings for young people to cuddle. But even more important, they presented an image of the flapper on the silver screen. In the early 1920s, almost 400 million people went to the movies every week. A study revealed that the young women who went to the movies "paid close attention to the star's appearance and behavior." Actresses such as Colleen Moore and Louise Brooks played flappers in story after story. Whether the character was a salesgirl in a lingerie department or a manicurist in a barber shop, she always met a young man. Her flapper character danced the Charleston and batted her dark-rimmed eyes teasingly. By the movie's end, however, the flapper had usually settled down, virtue intact. She turned out to be less permissive than her

A 1927 Life *magazine cover shows a flapper attempting to shift the gears of an automobile, thereby causing pieces of the vehicle to scatter across the road. A male police officer blocks out the grinding sound of the gears. The illustration is ironically captioned, "Shifting for Herself."*

clothing, dancing, or makeup suggested. And she usually married her young man.

Movies were make-believe stories that typically had happy endings. But what about in real life? If a flapper dressed in a risqué manner, did she also behave in a risqué way? Or did she dress the way she did—and paint her lips scarlet and ring her eyes with dark pencil—because it was a fad and she was just going along with the crowd? Was she like the Clara Bow characters who shocked their elders and teased young men but really were good girls?

Editor Bruce Bliven said in "Flapper Jane" that the clothing women wore on the streets of New York City were more revealing than that worn by any of the flappers he'd seen in the movies. Flappers certainly did what their mothers and especially their grandmothers had never done: rode in cars, kissed young men to whom they were not engaged, chewed gum, smoked, drank liquor, and used slang words such as *horsefeathers!* (meaning "darn") and "It's the cat's meow!" (meaning "wonderful").

Even so, Bliven believed that the flapper's costume was just a decoration she wore on the outside and not a real indication of her moral character. He wrote, "There is a good deal more smoke than fire."

The war, the Nineteenth Amendment, the automobile, and movies may all have had some influence on the flapper's rebellion. But more important, said Bliven, the flapper's dress and behavior were about control. After years of following social rules imposed upon them, usually by men, women were finally making up their own rules of what was acceptable and what was not. So what if they shaved their heads in defiance? he asked. He wrote: "Women have highly resolved that they are just as good as men, and intend to be

Colleen Moore's youth and fashion sense made her the typical flapper. Her first major role was in Flaming Youth *in 1923. It immediately made her one of the most popular actresses of the decade. Films and still photographs were shot in black and white at that time, so it did not matter that she had one brown eye and one blue one.*

The 1928 film Our Dancing Daughters *was a story about the natural tensions between the conservative cultural values of the 1800s and the freer, more open attitude toward sex and enjoyment of life that came after the end of World War I. The film starred* (from left to right) *Dorothy Sebastian, Joan Crawford, and Anita Page.*

Mrs. Grundy Fights Back

Mrs. Grundy had been overseeing conventional propriety (acceptable behavior) for a very long time. Originally a character from Thomas Morton's 1798 play *Speed the Plough,* she was an old woman of the middle or upper class who believed in the old moral code. A 1920s cartoon character, she looked with disgust upon the younger generation, most particularly the flapper. Emily Post warned her readers to beware of Grundy. She had the eyes of a hawk and the tongue of a magpie, a crowlike bird known for its chatter. Grundy was a snob, a snoop, and a gossip. Emily Post imagined this busybody living in an old Victorian home on a hill and spending her hours in the window with a periscope, a telescope, and a telephone. According to Emily Post, Grundy's whole purpose in life was to "track down and destroy the good name of every woman who comes within range, especially if she is young and pretty—and unchaperoned!"

Although Grundy was a myth, nothing more than a media image, plenty of real-life Grundys strolled Main Street. Grundys could also be found on the beach, where modern girls were causing shock waves by wearing one-piece bathing suits that revealed bare arms and legs instead of the customary layers of clothing, including

treated so. They don't mean to have any more unwanted children. They don't intend to be debarred from any profession or occupation which they choose to enter." He ended his article with a cheer for all the flappers: "Hurrah! Hurrah!"

Chicago police of the 1920s were assigned to protect public morals. They made sure that the rules about the distance between the bathing suit and the bather's knee were strictly observed.

bathing skirts with socks and shoes. On some beaches, police arrested these scantily dressed young ladies, either escorting them or (if they resisted) carrying them into paddy wagons for a trip to the police station.

Grundy and the fashion police were hard at work in the 1920s. Politicians in Utah proposed a new state law in 1921. Any woman who wore in public a skirt "higher than three inches [8 cm] above the ankle" could be arrested and imprisoned. A state bill in Virginia forbade "any woman from wearing shirtwaists or evening gowns which displayed more than three inches of her throat." Ohio's lawmakers were equally eager to outlaw clothing that accentuated a woman's figure. Not all of these bills became laws. Still, these proposals show a strong resistance to the women's modern clothing.

Mrs. John B. Henderson was a real-life Grundy. She was a member of the Washington, D.C., society, a tight circle of mostly wealthy women who were the wives of senators, congressmen, and diplomats. She was an art collector, who headed women's committees that sponsored art exhibits. Her name appeared often on the women's pages of newspapers in the nation's capital in the 1920s. Her name became known across the nation in 1926.

Women Make News: Fashion Feuds

The fictional Mrs. Grundy has been around for a long time. The name is traced to Thomas Morton's 1798 play Speed the Plough. *A new Mrs. Grundy seems to appear in each generation. She appoints herself the overseer of acceptable manners. The newspaper articles quoted here suggest that the 1926 version of Mrs. Grundy might have been Mrs. John B. Henderson* (above).

WASHINGTON — The international campaign to reform the extreme fashions of modern women and to "curb dissipation (self-indulgence) among them, such as cigarette-smoking, which is leading to degeneracy (corruption)," instituted here by Mrs. John B. Henderson received an official setback when the Female Bloc in the House of Representatives, composed of the three women members now occupying seats, voiced disagreement with the plan. Banding together for an official statement on the subject, the "gentlewomen" said they have no fear for the morality of young women so long as dresses remain below the knee. Mrs. Henderson's resolution branded the short skirt as a vulgar imitation of underworld fashions and said present day tendencies are destructive to . . . modesty, good taste and morals and that they imperil future health and efficiency.

—*International Herald Tribune,* January 9, 1926

WASHINGTON — The backwash has set in from every section of the country. It seems that Mrs. John B. Henderson, Washington society leader, is more to be pitied then censored for her efforts to lengthen the skirts of the young ladies of the land. The women of the country say they would be satisfied if skirts were lengthened just enough to hide the knees when the girls sit down. There is almost universal disapproval of Mrs. Henderson's ideas that skirts always should be of ankle length. That is going too far. A skirt midway between knees and ankles is favored by many experts on dress.

—*International Herald Tribune,* February 5, 1926

That was the year in which she began a "crusade for modesty." The goal of her crusade was to "call upon society women of America everywhere to band together to condemn" women's fashions that were vulgar and immodest.

"I never went downtown that I wasn't annoyed by the leg shows that I saw on every side of me," she told a reporter for the *New York Times*. "It wasn't only that the skirts were above the knees, but the sheer flesh-tinted stockings made the girls look as if their legs were absolutely naked."

The "leg shows" of Washington, D.C., also disturbed a good many of Henderson's social acquaintances, all women of upper society. None of these women, however, were willing to step forward to take action. The flappers, it seemed, had to be tolerated. That was not good enough for Henderson. "I soon saw that if anything was to be accomplished I should have to start moving on my own initiative," she said. Appointing herself moral guardian of women's fashions, she wrote a series of resolutions expressing her views and sent them to newspapers.

"The World War left us with our sense of values gone and our moral stamina weakened," she wrote. "The girls are shameless in dress and conduct alike." The situation was dire, she insisted. She even compared the United States in the 1920s to Rome in the corrupt days before the fall of the Roman Empire. She asked women everywhere to boycott the offending fashions.

During one interview, a reporter questioned Henderson about the length of skirts. They should be ankle length, she responded. Anything else was indecent. The feisty reporter reminded her that the president's wife, Mrs. Calvin Coolidge, wore skirts that were 10 inches (25 cm) from the ground. Henderson, the reporter wrote, seemed "pained." But with perfect composure, she responded, "Mrs. Coolidge is a woman of tremendous common sense. I have not seen her in all types of costume, but I have never seen her when her dress was not correct in every respect." She said, "Let's not pass judgment on her."

The Story of Johnny Hopeful and Miss Innocent

In 1922 Psychology Press published a book called *Fascinating Womanhood*. It was a how-to manual for young girls explaining the finer points of attracting a man and encouraging him to propose marriage. The title page lists no author, and so there is no way of knowing whether a man or a woman wrote the book. The author's point of view on the subject, however, is clearly expressed.

High-Heeled Contradictions

What could be more perfect and more painful for a flapper's night on the town than these patent leather high-heeled shoes with white straps and heels? And what could be more perfect and more practical for the new American woman's busy day than these comfy, health-enhancing Cantilevers?

Freedom from Foot Fatigue

DO you always enjoy your evenings—or are you often too tired? Does foot fatigue mar the hours which should be your happiest?

Nature designed your feet to serve as two tireless springs. They should carry you through the day with ease, leaving you fresh and ready for an evening of pleasure.

Shoes with rigid arches bring on foot fatigue by working against your feet all day long. Wrongly shaped shoes affect your bodily health by irritating important nerves and weakening the muscles of the feet and lower limbs. High heels thrust the body forward and often cause headache, backache and displacement of the internal organs. Shoes *are* important. Physicians know this and women are learning it.

The Cantilever Shoe is like the foot, shaped naturally and flexible from toe to heel. It is in close harmony with your foot in any position. Each step you take in a Cantilever Shoe is a foot exercise that strengthens the muscles which hold the bones of the foot in arched form. Strong, springy arches are the result of well-exercised foot muscles. Rigidly supported, the arches weaken because the foot muscles lack exercise. That is why you will find greater comfort and foot health in the flexible support of the snug-fitting, all-leather arch of the Cantilever Shoe.

The well placed, moderate heel of the Cantilever swings the body weight off the inner and weaker side of the foot and does not tilt the body forward at a harmful angle. The modishly rounded toe allows ample room for all five toes of the foot. The graceful, natural lines permit your foot to relax in comfort. And the unusual fitting qualities—the snug heel seat, the contoured arch, offer you the luxury of real foot comfort.

There are many smart models to select from this Autumn. A gored step-in pump, three-strap pumps, and distinctive designs in two-strap pumps offer a fine selection for dress occasions. For daytime wear there are several trim oxfords and snug boots.

If none of the dealers listed at the right is near you, write the manufacturers, Morse & Burt Co., 418 Willoughby Avenue, Brooklyn, N.Y., for the address of a nearer store.

Cantilever Shoe

At a meeting of the Housekeepers' Alliance in Washington, D.C., a group of three hundred housewives listened in awe as a local surgeon told them that high-heeled shoes were a "vile" invention of torture rather than fashion. They caused weakened arches, sprained ankles, corns, bunions, overlapping toes, rheumatism, and even stomach trouble. The surgeon (unnamed in the newspaper article) described having to amputate toes from patients as a result of their insistence on wearing narrow high-heeled shoes.

A few weeks later, however, the same newspaper reported a very different story. A doctor in Paris had concluded that high-heeled shoes could benefit a woman's health. How so? "High heels throw the weight of the body, while walking, on the tips of toes, thus exercising the muscles," the doctor explained. This, in turn, could prevent tuberculosis and other lung ailments.

Of course, not all women wore high-heeled shoes. Many wore sensible and safe Cantilevers. A cantilever is a type of support system, usually for the construction of a bridge or a balcony. One end of a projecting beam is solidly supported, while the opposite end is not. The cantilever construction distributes the weight evenly over the entire length. Cantilever shoes did much the same thing. The shoe's construction provided snug support at the heel. The arch of the shoe was flexible. Shoes with rigid arches could quickly tire feet muscles. Not the Cantilever! Advertisers promised busy women not only "freedom from foot fatigue," but also overall "happiness and better health." Busy women who wore them often worked in offices, department stores, or classrooms—jobs that required a great deal of time standing. Although Cantilevers were practical, many women thought they weren't very pretty. Many a flapper who danced the Charleston at night left her Cantilevers at home.

Women Make News in 1921: Margaret Gorman Crowned Miss America

She was just sixteen years old and a sharpshooter at marbles. Atlantic City loved her for her freckles and her long blonde ringlets, perhaps because she looked so very much like the sweetheart of silent films: actress Mary Pickford. Margaret Gorman, who lived in Washington, D.C., entered the first-ever Miss America beauty contest and swept the all-male judges off their feet.

The next morning, the *New York Times* reported on the United States' new patriotic beauty. Margaret Gorman was not a flapper. She was the country's "new American woman"—pretty and a little daring but wholesome.

The first Miss America pageant was a tourist gimmick created by businessmen in Atlantic City, New Jersey. The seaside resort was a popular family destination in the summer, but come the cooler months of autumn, the boardwalk was abandoned. The businessmen hoped a festival called Fall Frolic might lure people back to the beach. The beauty pageant was part of the festivities. The businessmen hoped that hundreds of beautiful young girls might enter by sending a photograph of themselves to the judges. Only a few dozen came to Atlantic City to compete. Nevertheless, they created a sensation!

Margaret Gorman was the very first Miss America. She does her best (above) *to lend a patriotic touch to a pageant that, in 1921, was nothing but an Atlantic City tourist draw.*

"For the time being, the censor ban on bare knees and skintight bathing suits was suspended," wrote an astonished reporter, "and thousands of spectators gasped as they applauded the girls."

The pageant was a glittering success for the Atlantic City businessmen, as more than

Along with her fellow contestants, Margaret Gorman (second from left) had agreed to the contest's only requirement: each beauty must appear in the parade revue wearing a bathing suit. It was a shocking idea at the time.

one hundred thousand people came into the city. The bathing beauties, too, got their share of fame. But the pageant also raised the hackles of women's groups and religious organizations across the country. Studying and comparing a woman's body parts was immoral, they insisted. The Young Women's Christian Association (YWCA) argued that the contest was "harmful in every way." The National Council of Catholic Women called the contest "a backward step in the civilization of the world." The *New York Times* on April 18, 1924, called the women's clothing "shocking."

Year after year, the parade of beauties on the boardwalk of Atlantic City continued. Each year the protests against it grew louder until at last the businessmen who dreamed up the pageant decided it might hurt business. People were beginning to speak of Atlantic City not as a family vacation spot but as a resort of risqué activities. In 1928 the city's businessmen canceled the beauty contest. (Although, in 1932, the pageant would return and remains an annual competition.)

Corinne Griffith (above) *starred in the 1924 silent film* Love's Wilderness. *In the film, her character appears very innocent but may actually be a stalker on the prowl.*

"Thoughtful-minded people have deplored the chaotic conditions which came as an aftermath of the Great War," the author writes in the introduction. The modern woman is flippant and arrogant and immodest in her dress and behavior. *Fascinating Womanhood* is a book that is "sorely needed," the author states, "a work that any good mother would be glad to place in the hands of her daughter."

The author claims to know the kind of woman every man wants—a woman who is tender, weak, and childlike. A woman's goal, the author tells the reader, is "to make yourself somebody's pet."

Dress in such a way as to be "huggable," the author suggests. "Too many women pay attention to the apparel itself and not to the impression the dress will make. . . . Would you hug a child in a soiled, tattered frock?" the author asks. "Or would you prefer the child in a lovely pink bonnet, soft organdie [fine, sheer fabric with a stiff finish] dress with little pink knees . . . dainty hair ribbons?"

Rather than viewing women as independent equals to men, the author uses language that reduces women to obedient pets and naive children. How the modern American women reacted to this book is hard to determine. But surely some women read the book eagerly for tips on how to land a husband, especially if she didn't consider herself beautiful. The author, in fact, makes a point of explaining that beauty "is not necessary" to tease a proposal of marriage from a man.

Teasing was the author's suggested strategy. The author outlines five steps in getting a man to propose. To illustrate how each step works, the author creates two fictional characters: Johnny Hopeful and Miss Innocent.

In stage one, Attracting Attention, Miss Innocent attends as many social events as possible where eligible men will be present. The author writes:

> Wherever a group of men can be found and the presence of girls can in any way be sanctioned [approved], there you will find Miss Innocent in all her glory. Not only does she advertise herself by appearing everywhere, but she also takes pains to appear her best. Her hair is always arranged in just the fashion most becoming to her; her complexion has just the right touch of cosmetics; and her attire, even if she had to be her own dressmaker, is always the most girlish and most cuddlesome to be found.

The author never explains what a "cuddlesome" dress might be—but "girlish" suggests that Miss Innocent does not flaunt bare chest or knees!

Demure as she may appear in her dress, Miss Innocent is on a mission, and it does not involve socializing with others. "While other girls are discussing sports or personalities, she is thinking of her appearance, fixing a stray hair, eyeing herself in the glass, or sizing up the men." She has come for one reason only, to catch the eye of a man. When she does, when he glances across the room at her, she responds in her girlish way: "She lets him catch her startled eyes, drops her lashes in pretty confusion, and, if possible, even engineers a blush."

Stage two is Arousing Interest. The gentleman has crossed the room to introduce himself. Miss Innocent says little about herself, however. Rather, she talks about Johnny. She listens wide eyed and oohs and aahs at Johnny's words. For example, if Johnny states that he swims, Miss Innocent should gasp in amazement. She might even ask her fellow how he can "keep from sinking"

Without missing a beat, Miss Innocent plays her next card: weakness. She could never swim, she claims. Why, she'd sink! In this way, she flatters Johnny so that he begins to believe that perhaps he is someone special simply because he can swim.

The third and fourth stages involve creating desire. Miss Innocent accomplishes this through more flattery. As Johnny Hopeful begins to tell Miss Innocent about himself and his desires, she oohs and aahs at each revelation, making him feel that he is admirable, "a better man than even he himself thought." Over time, Johnny Hopeful begins to feel that he cannot live without this approval.

The final stage is nursing Johnny's desire into a proposal. Miss Innocent does something completely unexpected. She encourages the attention of several other young men and avoids Johnny Hopeful. Once Johnny's jealousy rises to a boiling point, she agrees to see him. She arranges for a romantic location—the author recommends a lawn swing in a garden in the moonlight. Should Johnny accuse Miss Innocent of cheating on him, she begins to sob. He then feels that he's a brute. He apologizes first and proposes next.

Just how popular a book *Fascinating Womanhood* was in the 1920s is unclear. But the image it creates of young girls is very clear. Miss Innocent is not really childlike, weak, or even tender at all. She just pretends to be to achieve her goal—a husband.

"She lets him catch her startled eyes, drops her lashes in pretty confusion, and, if possible, even engineers a blush."

—from the 1922 book *Fascinating Womanhood*

The Duenna Is Watching!

In the barrio (Spanish-speaking neighborhood) of a small town in Arizona, the mothers of young girls chaperoned them at local dances. While the young men and women danced, the mothers—as well as some fathers—stood along the walls and watched. "They were always spying on us," said Ruby Estrada. But she added, "We took it in stride. It was taken for granted that that's the way it was."

In Mexican American communities, a chaperone, or duenna, accompanied young girls not only to dances but also to the movies and sometimes even to church activities. The chaperone might be an older sister or a maiden aunt. Chaperoning was a way for a family to protect young ladies from the temptations of modern life in the United States. A daughter's virtue reflected the family's honor. And so if a boy held a girl too close, the duenna might step forward and separate them. Words whispered too softly might also cause the duenna to cast a warning glance. Some rebellious modern senoritas plotted to "ditch the duenna" by sneaking out at night. If caught, an angry father might whip the girls.

Were boys as closely monitored as girls? Said one mother who had sons only and no daughters, "I do not have to worry," but she added, "the poor señoras with many girls, they worry."

Vicki Ruiz recalls her mother's stories of childhood. In her family, "there was no *dueña* because she was not allowed to date at all." Still, her mother found ways to have fun with her girlfriends or to secretly meet a boyfriend at the soda fountain of a local drugstore.

By 1933 things had not changed much according to Alice Leone Moats, who wrote in *No Nice Girl Swears*: "[A girl] needn't make an effort to appear brilliant—brains are a handicap to the debutante [young woman making a formal entrance into society], all she has to do is to look vastly interested and amused at everything her neighbor says and keep up a steady flow of adjectives when he pauses for breath."

Courting and Chaperones

It is wrong to believe that young women of the 1920s belonged to one of two categories: the wild-spirited flapper or the manipulative Miss Innocent. In fact, women's personalities and moral beliefs varied greatly. For every woman who was a flapper, there was one who wasn't.

Sennett's Bathing Beauties

Mack Sennett was a maker of movies in the 1920s. His slapstick comedies often involved cream pie fights, chaotic car chases, and bare-legged ladies in bathing suits. The bathing beauties were starlets, aspiring actresses. Sennett knew beautiful young women would attract moviegoers. His bathing beauties, however, also attracted hundreds of irate letters from community leaders and women's organizations that thought Sennett's showcasing of young, scantily dressed women was immoral. Even so, the bathing beauties were very popular and many of the starlets became full-fledged movie stars. Among the Hollywood actresses who slipped into a revealing bathing suit for a Mack Sennett comedy were Mabel Normand and Gloria Swanson.

Mack Sennett is mainly remembered as the head of the studio that produced slapstick comedies starring the Keystone Kops. He also tried to add a sense of glamour to the film industry. He produced a series of films featuring the Keystone Bathing Beauties, some of whom are shown here posing in automobile tires in the mid-1920s.

For every conniving Miss Innocent, there was a girl who was truly innocent and honest. Anne and Ernestine Gilbreth were two such girls. Their parents, Frank and Lillian Gilbreth, were efficiency experts. Industries hired them to study their factories, to identify the best ways to run them, and to save time, energy, and—most important—money. The Gilbreth parents applied their time-saving ideas to running their home as well. The goal at home wasn't to earn profits but to reduce the amount of time spent doing tasks, allowing more time for leisure activities—what the Gilbreths called "happiness moments."

Lillian and Frank Gilbreth were efficiency experts. They believed there was one best way of doing anything, whether it was assembling products in a factory or raising a family. At home the Gilbreth children often listened to French language records while brushing their teeth. That way, they could learn while keeping their teeth clean.

Frank Gilbreth was not a Mrs. Grundy, but he had definite ideas about how his young daughters should dress. He would not tolerate immodesty. Anne was the eldest daughter. When she was a senior in high school, she wanted to bob her hair. Her father would not allow it.

One afternoon, Anne closed the bathroom door behind her, lifted the scissors, and began to snip. When she stepped out, her long locks were gone. Ernestine was impressed that Anne had taken matters into her own hands. There was nothing their father could do. Still, she told her older sister her head looked at if she had backed into a lawn mower!

When Anne appeared at dinner that evening, Lillian Gilbreth was so startled by her daughter's transformation, she dropped the peas all over the table. Frank Gilbreth ordered Anne to remove that ridiculous wig. When he realized it wasn't a wig, he ordered her to grow her hair back—and fast! Anne fled the room in tears. Her mother, too, cried. Later, after tempers had calmed down, Anne returned. She and Ernestine used their parents' logic to explain why bobbed hair was better. It took less time to wash, dry, and style. Bobbed hair meant more leisure time for young girls. The Gilbreths couldn't argue with that. A few days later, Lillian took all six of her daughters to the barber and every-one got bobbed.

Compared to the long upswept hairstyles of the prior decade, the short bobs of the 1920s seemed masculine.

It took less time to wash, dry, and style.
Bobbed hair meant more leisure time for young girls.

Courting, on the other hand, posed an insurmountable challenge for Anne and Ernestine. When Joe Scales, a popular cheerleader (young men, not girls, were cheerleaders during the 1920s), asked Anne to the high school prom, her father pulled out his notebook and saw that he had no appointments for that evening. Anne understood that her father meant to chaperone her on her first real date. "Don't you trust your own flesh and blood?" she asked.

He did. It was the cheerleader he didn't trust. "Either I go," her father said, "or you don't."

On the night of the prom, Joe arrived in a Model T. Anne climbed into the front seat, and her father climbed into the back.

When Ernestine started dating soon after, Frank Gilbreth chaperoned her as well. When he couldn't, he sent her older brother along. For some young girls, having a chaperone while courting remained a way of life well into the 1920s.

"Blow Some My Way"

In the early years of the twentieth century, the Anti-Cigarette League of America crusaded to save young boys from the harmful effects of tobacco. The group did not worry about young girls simply because girls did not smoke. Some women did smoke in the years before the Great War, but they usually did so in the privacy of their home. In public, middle- or upper-class women did not put cigarettes to their pure mouths. Nor did a gentleman light up a cigar or cigarette in the presence of a woman without first asking her permission—at least not according to Emily Post's rules of etiquette and proper behavior.

Even among gentlemen, smoking was a controversial habit. Medical science had not yet proven that smoking was dangerous at all—much less how very dangerous it was. Yet there must have been some suspicion. Slang phrases for cigarettes during these early years of the twentieth century included "devil's toothpicks," "coffin nails," and "little white slavers." In 1914 inventor Thomas

Edison sent a persuasive letter to automobile manufacturer Henry Ford about the harmful effects of tobacco: Addressing his letter to "Friend Ford," he wrote:

> *The injurious agent in cigarettes comes principally from the burning paper wrapper. The substance thereby formed, is called "Acrolein." It has a violent action on the nerve centers, producing degeneration of the cells of the brains, which is quite rapid among boys.*

The brain damage, said Edison, was permanent. He ended his letter with a firm statement:

"I employ no person who smokes cigarettes." Neither did Henry Ford; Sears®, Roebuck and Company; or Montgomery Ward.

During the Great War, however, cigarettes became a cheap and easy way of shipping tobacco to U.S. troops overseas. Even the American Red Cross sent cartons of cigarettes to the soldiers, based on the opinion of doctors that tobacco provided soothing relief to pain and could ease nervousness.

After the war, the popularity of cigarettes continued. Youth, in particular, took up the habit. A shocked older generation protested.

Gimme a Little Kiss, Baby Face!

Popular music and song lyrics of the 1920s reflected the carefree and optimistic spirit of the times. The invention of radio popularized the music, broadcasting it into homes across the United States.

The music also reflected the changing roles of women, especially in their relationships with the men who courted them. In "Baby Face," the young man has fallen in love: "My poor heart is jumping, You sure have started something." In "If You Knew Susie," the love-stricken man sings about his lassie's "chassie" (body). "Oh, Oh, Oh what a gal!" he exclaims. Another popular song from 1926, "Gimme a Little Kiss," suggested women were coy with the boys. A fellow pleads with his girl to give him a kiss or at least a squeeze. "Gosh oh gee, why do you refuse?" he argues. "I can't see what you gonna lose." One recording of this song used sound effects, including a smoochy kiss and slap!

In the early twentieth century, the phonograph and recorded music began to grow in importance, competing with sheet music. Once the radio became popular in the 1920s, the sales of sheet music began a slow decline. Eventually the music industry would sell far more records than sheet music.

Many middle-class homes had a piano. Thousands of music stores across the country sold sheet music for these popular songs. Sometimes the artist who sang the song appeared on the cover of the sheet music. Often the image was of a woman. It might be a flapper wrapped in a coat with a mink collar or chatting on a telephone. It might also be a college coed dancing the Charleston or baring her shoulder and looking provocatively off the page.

The song titles often referred to women affectionately as "baby." Consider these popular hits from the 1920s: "When My Baby Smiles at Me," "Everybody Loves My Baby," and "I Found a Million Dollar Baby (in a Five and Ten Cent Store)." While *baby* was supposed to be an expression of affection, the word also suggests an immature person who needs parenting, or at least a man to take care of her.

"Women of judgment and sense . . . are all dead set against the tobacco habit," stated a spokesperson for the Methodist Church in a magazine article. "It will die after a brief vogue, with a few fools who, like moths, have not sense enough to keep from singeing themselves at the flame." The "moths," however, kept smoking. Smoking cigarettes would prove not to be a passing fad but an addiction.

Women began smoking cigarettes for much the same reason as they bobbed their hair, shortened their skirts, and painted their lips. Smoking was an outward symbol of rebellion, a way of shunning their parents' old code of moral behavior. Initially, advertisers did not market their products to women. Women smokers were controversial. The tobacco manufacturers feared that advertisements might trigger a negative reaction. After all, Prohibition groups had worked effectively to ban alcohol. Groups such as the Anti-Cigarette League of America might try to make smoking illegal.

The first advertisements to target women smokers began in the mid-1920s. "Blow Some My Way" was the name of an advertisement for Chesterfield cigarettes. In one image, a woman sits on rock near a lake, her arms linked around her knees. Next to her is a man lighting a cigarette. The trail of smoke drifts away from her. She is looking at him or perhaps at the smoke. The line "Blow some my way" is set in quotation marks, suggesting the woman has spoken this.

Advertisements work on two levels: text and subtext. Text is the literal meaning of the words and images. Subtext is the figurative, or suggested, meaning. In "Blow Some My Way," the way the woman leans toward the man, looking at him, suggests that the trail of smoke is not offensive at all. Her line of dialogue suggests that women wish they, too, could smoke. At a time when cigarettes were referred to as

> Women began smoking cigarettes for much the same reason as they bobbed their hair, shortened their skirts, and painted their lips.

devil's toothpicks, this advertising image was quite a sensation.

Did the advertisement persuade women to smoke? Or was it simply mirroring what many women were already doing? About the same time that the Chesterfield ads appeared in magazines, young college women were demanding the right to smoke on campus. Smoking wasn't a moral decision, the female students argued. It was simply "a matter of taste," a personal decision about an activity they found pleasurable. Pennsylvania's Bryn Mawr College in 1925 was the first to grant smoking rights to its female students. Four more years would pass, however, before women at Ohio State University got the same right.

Taking note of the change on college campuses, tobacco manufacturers began hiring advertisers to create campaigns targeting women. "Reach for a Lucky Instead of a Sweet" was the creative inspiration of Albert Lasker. He got the idea from his wife. Like many women during the 1920s, she was conscious of her weight. The new flapper styles emphasized a slim and flat-chested body. Dieting was one solution. Her doctor suggested another. As Albert Lasker recalled, "This doctor proposed to my wife . . . that before each meal, or between meals when she got hungry, she light a cigarette and then throw it away. He said that the smoke in the saliva would kill the appetite for a little while."

" **Bet you twenty**
you don't hole it! "

"Twenty what?"
"Twenty Kenilworths, of course!" War has made no difference to Kenilworth Cigarettes. In size, in shape, in excellence of packing and material, in flavour, in quality,

Kenilworths are still the same wonderful cigarettes you enjoyed "before the War."
Ask for Kenilworths by name, and make sure of getting the real thing in Virginian Cigarettes.

*The price of Kenilworth Cigarettes has had to be advanced by **2d.** for each 20. This is the absolute minimum that must be added so that the weight and fine quality of Kenilworth Cigarettes may be fully maintained. And they are being maintained to-day, as always. Kenilworth Cigarettes compare favourably with any cigarettes you can obtain—at any price.*
20 for 1|6 ; 50 for 3|8 ; 100 for 7|4.

Kenilworth Cigarettes

COPE BROS. & CO., LTD.,
LIVERPOOL AND LONDON.
Manufacturers of High-class Cigarettes.

Immediately after the Great War, cigarette ads began to subtly target women. They didn't show them smoking yet, but this woman is assuring her man that these are the same great cigarettes he enjoyed before the war. The viewer can only assume she's tried them herself.

She thought the idea was horrifying. She was not a rebellious college girl. Albert Lasker urged his wife to give it a try. Apparently the cigarette trick worked. Soon after, Lasker applied the same idea to an advertisement he created for the manufacturers of Lucky Strike cigarettes. His subtext would link weight loss with smoking. "Reach for a Lucky instead of a Bon Bon" was the first draft of the text. But Lasker nixed it because most Americans were not familiar with the French word for candy. "Reach for a Lucky instead of a candy" was better, but Lasker was still not satisfied. "We want people not to take pies and cakes," he said. And so, "sweet" replaced "bon bon" and advertising history was made. The sale of Lucky Strike cigarettes soared from $12 million a year in 1926 to $40 million in 1930. In just four years, Albert Lasker's campaign had helped to make Lucky Strike the best-selling cigarette in the country.

A large number of those new customers were women—and not just young college women. "The women broke the prejudice down overnight and began smoking in public," said Lasker. The "Blow Some My Way" advertisement became obsolete. If a woman wanted to smoke, she could simply light up for herself rather than staring longingly at a male and inhaling secondhand smoke. As the prejudice dwindled away, advertising images showed women holding cigarettes.

Other social factors also contributed to women smoking in public. Public relations specialist Edward Bernays created a sensation when he encouraged young women from the best social families to march in an Easter parade in New York City holding lit "torches of freedom." By calling the cigarettes torches, Bernays linked smoking with the new American woman's quest for equality with men. By placing these torches between the fingertips of high society women, Bernays played on ordinary women's desires to do as high society does. Movie fans also began imitating their favorite stars, who frequently smoked in scenes on the silver screen.

chapter four

beauty
in the
eye
of the
beholder

I mean to be attractive as long as I live—by keeping well. I have no patience with the woman who is sweetly resigned to being old at forty. She should be still a girl—splendidly alive and at the height of her beauty.

—Lifebuoy soap advertisement, *Good Housekeeping*, April 1924

some unusual fashions to enhance their bodies. In the eighteenth century, women wore "pocket hoops" to make their hips appear larger. The hoops were like baskets that the women tied underneath long skirts. So wide were the hips with these fashionable contraptions that women sometimes had to step sideways through a door. In the nineteenth century, the padding shifted from the hips to the buttocks as women wore bustles to exaggerate their backsides. The big bottom bustles gave women's bodies an S shape. Corsets allowed women—or rather their maids—to lace and squeeze their waists tightly to make them appear tiny. This beauty innovation gave women's bodies an hourglass shape.

In the 1920s, the S and hourglass shapes were no longer in style. Instead, the ideal silhouette was straight and slim. Because skirts were shorter, the visual interest was not the breasts, the hips, or the waist but rather a woman's legs. For some women, especially

THE MORNING NEG-LIGE is specially designed as a bridal peignoir. The Chemisette is only apparent, being really a portion of the garment. It is wrought in needle-work so as to give the garment the appearance of being a half-high dress. The sleeves are similarly constructed, so as to present the appearance of under-sleeves. If desired, the skirt may be wrought in a suitable design in needle-work, en quille. The corsage is close, and, with the skirt, is similar to that presented last month, being cut in one length, so as to fit rather closely at the waist, with a moderate fullness below. Our illustration is designed for white muslin. Should merino be selected for the material, a blue-bird egg color is appropriate, if it suits the complexion. In this case the robe must have the neck cut square, half-high, with an inside fichu; the sleeves also must be short, and turned back, buttoning upon themselves, with undersleeves arranged in broad plaits, as represented in the illustration. The vandyked sleeve-cap, which have buttons at each point, may be slightly stiffened. The cord and tassels are merely for ornament. The coiffure consists of a simple lace handkerchief.

The BOY'S TOILET consists of a Scotch cap of black velvet with feather and plaid band; a Zouave jacket; full trunk pants, closed at the knee, with over-alls and gaiters. The jacket is of dark-green velvet, heavily embroidered, and confined with hooks and eyes. It may be edged with gold lace.

The CHILD'S TOILET is of white muslin, trimmed with blue ribbons.

The CORSET TOURNURE is a novelty which is highly recommended. While serving the purpose indicated by its name, it forms an effectual support for the skirts.

We also illustrate a SKIRT SUPPORTER, the extreme lightness and simplicity of which commends it to public favor. It consists of a girdle of three parallel slips of watch-spring steel, furnished with a slide so as to be readily adapted to the size of the wearer; this, instead of the person of the wearer, receives the pressure of the girding; small protuberances projecting from the girdle serve as points of supports for the skirts. This girdle, with the

FIGURE 4.—CORSET TOURNURE

skirts, is sustained by light braces passing over the shoulder.

FIGURE 5.—SKIRT SUPPORTER

No. 6. WINTER PELISSE.

his novel cloak combines the small dolman, with a waterfall back,

NOTICE.

Each pair bears the Registered Number, and can only be obtained at 256, Regent St.

"THE ABDOMINAL CORSET." Regd. 32801.

.ite Coutille, Low Bust ... 24 6   White Coutille, High Bust ... 26 9

The styles of undergarments and dresses of the late 1800s and early 1900s camouflaged women's natural shapes. The illustrations above are from the late 1800s. Facing page: Flapper fashion, on the other hand, did not disguise the female form.

those who were large busted or overweight, the new flapper style of dressing posed a problem. Some of these women began wrapping their breasts to appear flat chested. Rubber girdles could likewise flatten the stomach and hips. But what of fat calves and swollen ankles? These were more challenging problems. One solution was reducing, or dieting.

thin is in

What's for dinner?

Before the Great War, the average middle- or upper-class American family dined on steak, roasts, macaroni, potatoes, turnips, apples, and stewed tomatoes. For dessert they might have rice pudding, cake, or pie. Perhaps not every American family ate all these foods at one sitting, but a study completed by social researchers Helen and Robert Lynd documented that the American dinner table was heavy with food. By the mid-1920s, however, the United States' upper class had curbed their appetite. Breakfast was eggs and cereal. Lunch was soup and a sandwich. Dinner might be steak or a roast but not both. Fresh fruits and vegetables were more likely to be placed upon the table.

Why were Americans changing their diets? New kitchen appliances and convenience foods (such as canned vegetables and soups) were one reason. Women's magazines with their tips on what to eat were another. Still another factor was a change in attitude. Before the war, most Americans associated excess weight with prosperity. Only a wealthy person could afford to serve three different meats at dinner! In contrast, skinny people were poor and probably unhealthy. After the war, however, Americans' idea of what was beautiful changed.

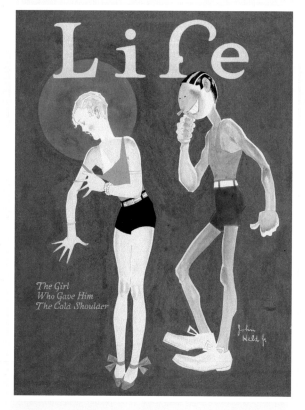

The heavy corsets and long skirts of the 1910s were a thing of the past. Clingy fabrics, short skirts, and very revealing bathing costumes, as in this Life *cover from 1923, put women of the 1920s into a weight-loss mode.*

The One O'Clock Luncheon

In the 1920s, many manufacturers of food products produced recipes booklets as a way of advertising their products to American housewives. The minicookbooks reinforced the company's brand name, such as JELL-O. They also provided instruction for young housewives on how to use the new mass-produced food products in their menus. "In the good old days," stated an advertising booklet for Carnation *(below)*, "practically every family 'kept a cow.'" Those days were gone. In the 1920s, canned milk was a popular convenience and Carnation's cookbook provided recipes for housewives while ensuring they were using a quality ingredient.

In the 1920s, Calumet baking powder also produced an advertising booklet. "A woman longs for new culinary worlds to conquer," the author stated in the introduction. "She wearies of the same kind of biscuits, the cake she learned to make for her first grown up party, the old way of serving chicken." Calumet's recipes for "The One O'Clock Luncheon" listed the following menu: sardine canapés with gherkin pickles, chicken shortcake (creamed chicken and mushrooms served over a biscuit), pineapple salad, chocolate ice cream, and macaroons. Everything was homemade, even the ice cream. Most importantly, the recipes included a few teaspoonfuls of Calumet baking powder.

Peppered throughout the booklet were interesting, scientific facts about the baking powder, such as "Calumet uses six million, five hundred thousand egg whites each year to produce its powder." That was very important information for the scientifically-oriented new American woman! She needed a lot of facts in order to justify her using these new, more expensive packaged products.

The Evils of Going Corsetless

Leonard Florsheim was the vice president of the Corset and Brassiere Association. In 1921 he wrote an article titled "The Evils of the No-Corset Fad." He used racial stereotypes to persuade middle- and upper-class white women that going corsetless was much the same as going wild. He painted a dire picture of what happens to the slim, youthful figures of women of various ethnic groups who don't choose to wear corsets when they are young.

That same year, an equally insulting article appeared with this headline: "Parisian Women Wear Corsets." It went on to suggest that American women who lost their shape by childbearing should be like chic French women, who wore corsets.

Additional articles and advertisements preyed on women's fear of aging and illness. Corsets could slow aging and prevent disease, the corset manufacturers claimed.

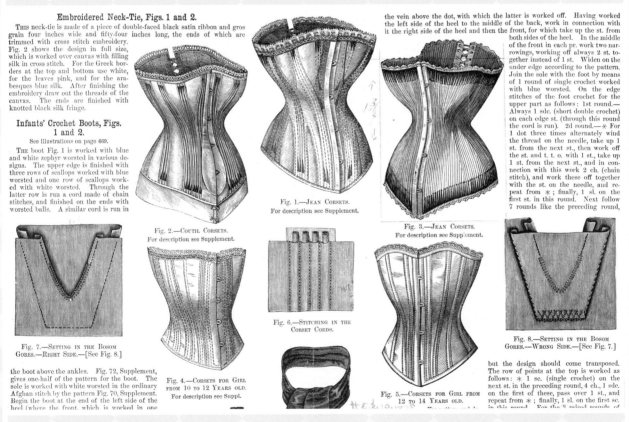

Women in the 1800s wore a stiff, firm undergarment called a corset. The corset ad above is from an 1878 edition of Harper's Bazaar *magazine. Even young girls at that time were encouraged to wear corsets to create a waistline. (Note that the corset on the lower right is labeled "Corsets for Girl from 12 to 14 years old," and the one on the lower left is labeled "Corsets for Girl from 10 to 12 years old"!)*

A stout, or corpulent, person was most likely unhealthy. Besides, a flapper's short skirt did nothing for an overweight woman.

No wonder then that in 1923, *Diet and Health, with Key to the Calories* was a best seller. The book by Dr. Lulu Hunt Peters, written for a female audience, was the first best-selling diet book.

After the war, however, Americans' idea of what was beautiful changed. A stout, or corpulent, person was most likely unhealthy. Besides, a flapper's short skirt did nothing for an overweight woman.

It remained on the best-seller's list for four years. In the book, readers met some corpulent characters: Mrs. Ima Gobbler, Mrs. Sheesasite, Mrs. Tiny Wyaton, and Mrs. Knott Little. Peters made up the names to be humorous, but her message was quite serious. She wrote:

> *Fat individuals have always been considered a joke, but you are a joke no longer. Instead of being looked upon with friendly tolerance and amusement, you are now viewed with distrust, suspicion, and even aversion!. . . You are in despair about being anything but fat, and—how you hate it. But cheer up. I will save you; yea, even as I have saved myself and many, many others.*

As a physician, Peters understood that the number of calories consumed versus the number of calories spent through exercise determined a woman's weight. As a woman who herself had weighed more than 200 pounds (90 kg) before dieting, she also understood the emotional trauma of being overweight. "How any one can want to be anything but thin is beyond my intelligence," she wrote.

Peters took a scientific approach to reducing. She warned her readers that reducing would not be easy. The dieting woman faced obstacles, the first of which was likely to be her husband. He will tell you, she wrote, that he does not like thin women. She added, "I almost hate my husband when I think how long he kept me under that delusion. Now, of course, I know all about his jealous disposition, and how he did not want me to be attractive."

the dieting woman faced obstacles,
the first of which was likely to be her husband.
He will tell you, Dr. Peters wrote,
that he does not like thin women.

The second obstacle, she said, was family and friends who insisted that a fatter woman looks younger and healthier. They might argue that losing weight could lead to a physical decline, even death! Don't believe it, Peters stated. She also warned her readers to ignore the quackery of so many advertisements that promised weight loss through pills or other antifat medicines. They were dangerous. Some contained substances poisonous to the human body, such as arsenic and mercury.

Most colleges addressed the issue of weight control as part of women's health education. At Smith College, a highly respected all-female college in Northampton, Massachusetts, the students who studied Food I learned about calories and balancing their diet.

Coco Chanel and Real Chic

Gabrielle "Coco" Chanel didn't invent the bobbed hairstyle for women. But in bobbing her own hair, the French designer popularized the fashion trend. As the story goes, one afternoon a gas hot water heater in Chanel's home exploded. Soot caked her long, dark hair. Chanel reached for scissors before reaching for the soap. She was going to the opera that evening. When Chanel appeared, she had a simple ribbon tied around her bobbed hair—and she created a sensation.

In 1921 Chanel, shown here in 1919, introduced a sophisticated non-floral-smelling perfume that she called simply No. 5. "Women are not flowers. Why should they want to smell like flowers?" she asked.

Gabrielle Chanel's mother died when she was quite young, and Chanel lived for a time in an orphanage. She shocked the nuns there when she gave up her seamstress job to become a singer on the stage of a cabaret. She adopted Coco as her stage name. Her entertainment career didn't work. After a time, Chanel opened a hat shop in Paris and then a branch in the resort town of Deauville, France. In the early years of the twentieth century, women wore enormous, elaborate hats with brims full of feathers and silk flowers. Chanel thought they were ridiculous. "How can a brain function under those things?" she asked. In contrast, her hats were simple, snug, and uncluttered.

Chanel had no love of ribbons, bows, and lace—trimmings that she called, "fussy bits and pieces." She didn't much care for silk or crinoline, either. A modern woman drove automobiles, played golf, and worked in offices, and she couldn't do these things in silks and crinolines. Besides, those abrics were expensive. Far more affordable was jersey knit. When Chanel designed a loose-fitting jersey sweater and tied a belt around it, she shocked the fashion world. Woolen jersey was a fabric used most frequently to make men's underwear! In Chanel's hands, however, the jersey hung softly and didn't wrinkle. The fabric was comfortable, and women could move easily while wearing it.

Chanel was more than a trendsetter. She was a smart businesswoman. What had begun as a small hat-shop business soon grew into the House of Chanel in Paris. Coco Chanel would continue to influence women's fashion throughout the century.

The soap companies were among the first to aim their advertisements at specific buyers. Using a good soap could help the businesswoman (left) succeed—or it could help the married homemaker (right) keep her husband happy.

They studied about protein, minerals, and vitamins. The college professor linked weight control and balanced diet with good health. The students' interest in food, however, went beyond what was required to earn a passing grade. In the 1920s, college women—white college women, in particular—began to associate thinness with beauty. They talked about their bodies and weighed themselves frequently, recording in their diaries their disappointment when they gained pounds. They anxiously compared their weight to that of other girls on campus. Mary Fessenden, a student at Cornell University in New York, wrote home to her mother that she was angry with herself. She weighed 120 pounds (54 kg), one pound more than her friend. At Smith College, Lucy Kendrew wrote to her mother, "I had the worst scare the other day. . . . I weighed myself . . . & weighed 136? [62 kg]!"

In the 1920s, college women—white college women, in particular—began to associate thinness with beauty.

The boyish flapper look of the 1920s was only one reason why so many women became concerned with their weight. Another reason, also linked to fashion, was standardized sizing. In the nineteenth century and even the early years of the twentieth century, most women sewed their own clothing. Many went to a dressmaker who customized the clothing according to the woman's measurements. A common object in many households was a dress form, a headless mannequin built according to the owner's body measurements. The women fitted the dress she was sewing on the mannequin and adjusted the garment for fit.

In the years following the Great War, however, clothing manufacturers standardized sizing. Each size had specific dimensions. In this way, the manufacturers could mass-produce clothing more quickly and earn more profits. The result of the new "ready-to-wear" clothing, however, was that women suddenly had to fit one of the standard sizes. Those who did not often felt odd, even embarrassed—especially if they were trying on clothes in a department store dressing room where other women, including saleswomen, could see their flaws.

Other factors contributed to women's sudden interest in dieting. Women were unlacing and tossing away their uncomfortable corsets. Why? Corsets limited a woman's movement. In a corset, a woman could not play tennis, swim, ride a bike, or dance the Charleston or the turkey trot—at least not comfortably. Without a corset, however, any excess pounds were more obvious.

Corset sales dropped, though not dramatically. Nevertheless, the manufacturers of these women's undergarments waged a campaign to woo the ladies back. They designed lighter, more flexible corsets. The H. & W. Company of New York City created the elastic tape girdle "For Every Wear Everywhere." This new style girdle (*corset* apparently sounded too old-fashioned in the decade of the flapper) promised to give a woman a youthful figure while allowing greater freedom of movement.

from painted faces to beauty treatments

Mirrors were everywhere in the early decades of the twentieth century—in homes, dressing rooms and, in the 1920s, inside the nifty little flip-open compacts that women carried in their purses. A woman found it difficult not to look at herself in a mirror. At every turn of a magazine's page, advertisers and editors were encouraging her to stop, look, and evaluate her image.

Helen Lansdowne Resor was the head of advertising for the women's department at the J. Walter Thompson advertising agency in New York City. She had begun working in advertising as a secretary after graduating from high school. She had talent for more than typewriting and filing. She understood how to communicate to women through images and words. She soon became a copywriter, creating advertisements that appeared in newspapers and magazines. By the 1920s, she had become the most influential woman in advertising.

Resor was among the first copywriters to use sex appeal in advertising. Perhaps her most famous advertisement was for Woodbury facial soap. In this media image, a handsome man in a tuxedo is embracing a woman. His fingers are caressing her bare arm. She is looking away from him toward the audience. The headline was suggestive: "A skin you love to touch." Once Resor had caught the attention of her female readers, she proceeded to explain within the advertising text why they should purchase Woodbury soap:

Your skin, as it is now, is not a lifetime possession by any means. If you have thought so, you have overlooked this big fact: Your skin, like the rest of your body, is changing every day! As old skin dies, new skin forms. This is your opportunity. By using the proper external treatment, you can make this new skin just what you would love to have it.

Look closely, the advertisement implies. Is *your* skin dying? Would a man caress *your* bare arms?

Soap was just one ticket to a radiant complexion. Cosmetics were another. Face paints had long existed, concocted mostly from plants, including flowers, fruits, roots, and bark. In the nineteenth century, however, the painted lady was a "hussy," an immoral woman. Makeup reddened the lips and the cheeks. Hussies applied it for one reason only: to draw attention to themselves and so entice men's interest and their money.

Perhaps one reason why people looked at red lips and cheeks with scorn and even disgust is that for centuries, diseases such as tuberculosis had reddened the skin. Clear, unblemished skin was rare and so considered beautiful. Also, ruddy or reddened skin was often the result of working outdoors. In contrast, fair, untanned skin suggested a better social class, one that enjoyed leisure rather than laboring for a living.

Just as attitudes about corpulence had changed in the twentieth century, so, too, did attitudes about makeup. Mabel Williams was a young woman when her brother spied her applying a homemade mixture of petroleum jelly and coal dust to her eyelashes. The shiny jelly made Mabel's eyelashes appear longer. Some stories say that Mabel darkened her eyelashes to attract the attention of a young man. She may or may not have won his affections, but she did inspire her brother to create a new type of beauty product called mascara. T. L. Williams mixed coal dust with petroleum jelly, added a brush for application, and called it Maybelline. He advertised the ten-cent cakes of mascara in movie magazines and newspapers.

Mabel darkened her eyelashes to attract the attention of a young man. She may or may not have won his affections, but she did inspire her brother to create a new type of beauty product called mascara.

Other ambitious women had also begun to experiment with creams, waxes, rouges, and lipsticks. Helena Rubinstein and Elizabeth Arden both created vast cosmetic empires. Their first challenge was to convince middle- and upper-class women that makeup was not a vice but a virtue.

"There are no ugly women, only lazy ones," said Helena Rubinstein, implying that a plain woman lacked the energy and motivation to take better care of herself. To help women overcome their slothfulness, Helena Rubinstein—or Madame, as she preferred to be called—created a Day of Beauty. A woman who visited one of her salons could choose from a variety of treatments meant to cleanse and exfoliate the skin and increase circulation. She could soak in milk, mineral water, or herbs. She might stand under a needle-sharp shower or endure a pumice rub. She might lie quietly while a beautician applied electrical currents to her face or encased her in mud.

Elizabeth Arden emphasized the virtue of purity to sell her products. In the 1920s, she hired a French model and bandaged her head in white gauze to cover her hair and thus emphasize her beautiful face, especially her large eyes. The tight gauze wrapping looked as if a doctor had bandaged the head. The image suggested a medical procedure and not a beauty treatment. That was intentional. Elizabeth Arden wanted women to believe that beauty was a science and that her products were medical in nature. But the image was also strikingly different from any other beauty advertisement. The model resembled a nun. Elizabeth Arden loved the image because, she said, it suggested purity. She used the image to promote her products.

the soap-and-water women

Not all women in the 1920s used cosmetics. Those who did not were often referred to as soap-and-water women. The phrase had been in use since the nineteenth century. Then it meant a woman of honest virtue. In modern times, however, it had come to mean something a bit more negative: plainness and old-fashioned values.

DEMEYER

BRING YOUR IDEAL
to *Elizabeth Arden*

YOUR ideal—you know her almost better than yourself. And she's a dangerous lady to have about the house. She stands beside you every day before your mirror—with her you compare your reflection—because of her you see every flaw. No woman should harbor such a depressing companion!

Bring her to Elizabeth Arden . . . entrust your problem to the skillful hands, the wise mind that have given so much beauty to women.

First tell Miss Arden all you can about her—her carriage, the turn of her head, her loveliness of skin and eyes and hair. Then relax, in the comforting certainty that something is going to be done about her.

You'll find it an adventurous affair as the changes begin to show. Was it a sad tale the tape measure told about your waistline? Carefully directed exercise and massage are changing that. A dangerous hint of relaxation about your cheeks or chin? The Ardena Firming Treatments are proving their worth. A depressing little smudge beneath your eyes or just general tonelessness? Miss Arden has a specific treatment for each and every one.

Every day you will have one thing less to envy the woman you wish you were. Miss Arden's methods are so natural—so accurate, that clients who follow her faithfully need never accept less than genuine loveliness. Come to the Elizabeth Arden Salons . . . Let Miss Arden banish your shadowy rival once and for all.

*For an appointment at the hour you prefer,
please telephone Plaza 5847.*

ELIZABETH ARDEN
NEW YORK: 691 FIFTH AVENUE

RIS · LONDON · BERLIN · MADRID · ROME · BIARRITZ · C

The white wrappings and the tool being used on the face of the model in this cosmetics ad suggest a medical or surgical procedure. The image gives scientific appeal to Elizabeth Arden's beauty treatments.

Behind the Red Door

Elizabeth Arden did not have beauty parlors. Instead, she opened a series of high-class day spas in cities around the world. The door to each spa was painted a vivid, glossy red. A woman who stepped through the door was assured to be pampered—for a price, of course. First, she entered an oval waiting room, sumptuously decorated in white and gold. A beautician met with her to assess her cosmetic strengths and flaws and to make recommendations for treatment. Next, the woman slipped into a "withdrawing" room painted in sugary pastels. Here, she changed out of her street clothing and into a robe provided for her. Then the beauty treatment began.

For some treatments, such as the Vienna face mask, a nurse was in attendance. The presence of a nurse suggested that the cosmetic treatment was much more than window dressing for a woman's face. The beauticians weren't medically trained, but they dressed as if they were nurses—in white uniforms and white shoes. Instead of a nurse's cap, however, they wore a pink ribbon in their hair.

In an era when wearing makeup was considered acceptable only for stage performers, Elizabeth Arden (above) made cosmetics acceptable. She also made it an important part of good grooming for every woman who cared about her appearance.

It was science and, therefore, sure to produce results. Whether it was science or show biz, one thing is sure: the red doorway to beauty earned Elizabeth Arden not just wealth but fame around the world.

The Unmentionable

Women at the beginning of the twentieth century knew nothing about sanitary napkins simply because they had not yet been invented. Most women used strips of cloth during their menstrual cycles. They washed and reused the cloths each month. During the Great War, however, nurses dressed soldier's wounds with a new type of cotton padding made from wood fibers. These bandages were very absorbent and clean. The nurses improvised. They adapted the pads into "napkins" for use during their menstrual cycles. They discarded the napkins after use. However, disposing of the pad could be problematic and embarrassing. Instructions for flushable pads instructed users to remove the filling, rip the gauze wrapping in pieces and soak in the toilet's water before flushing. It was a messy and time-consuming task. Even when women followed the instructions, the thick padding often stopped-up the plumbing.

By 1920 the Kimberly-Clark company was manufacturing the napkins under the name Kotex. Menstruation, however, was not a topic discussed in popular women's magazines. Although natural, menstruation was an unmentionable part of a woman's life. So the company packaged Kotex in plain wrapping paper and sold it in pharmacies.

In 1921 the first Kotex advertisement appeared. Graceful, beautiful women appeared in these advertisements. The copy did not include the words *menstruation, women's cycle,* or *bleeding.* Instead, the language focused on daintiness, cleanliness, and hygiene. Women had to figure out what the product was. By the 1930s, the advertisements became a bit more direct. Even so, the napkins themselves did not appear in the ads. Instead, beautiful women, such as model Lee Miller, were photographed in evening gowns to advertise the product.

KOTEX

How War Nurses Found a New Use for Cellucotton

5¢ Each 12 for 60¢

NECESSITY being the mother of invention, our war nurses in France first discovered a new use for Cellucotton, which has led to Kotex—a universal product at a universal price.

"Cellucotton," they wrote, "is doing such wonderful work as a sanitary absorbent, that nurses are making sanitary pads from it for their own uses."

Thus when war ended, our laboratory developed the nurses' idea. For over two years experiments went on in preparing and also in marketing the new sanitary pads known as KOTEX—named from "cotton-like texture"—with the result that Kotex are now offered at a price every woman can afford in stores and shops that cater to women.

Kotex are more absorbent, cool, of lasting softness, cheap enough to throw away.

If KOTEX are not yet on sale in your neighborhood, write us for the names of nearest stores and shops that have them. Or send us sixty-five cents and we will mail you one box of a dozen Kotex in plain wrapper, charges prepaid.

CELLUCOTTON PRODUCTS CO.
208 South La Salle Street, Chicago, Illinois

INEXPENSIVE, COMFORTABLE, HYGIENIC and SAFE — KOTEX

A 1921 ad in Cosmopolitan *focuses on the early history of sanitary napkins. The ad states that the name Kotex came from the product's cottonlike texture. The featured selling point was a totally new concept—the pads were inexpensive enough to actually be thrown away.*

The manufacturers of Pond's had come to the J. Walter Thompson agency and Helen Lansdowne Resor, in particular, because their sales were down. Resor felt that the heart of the problem was that modern women associated Pond's with the negative image of the soap-and-water women. Women had been using Pond's Extract and Pond's Cold Cream since before the American Civil War (1861–1865). That, too, was part of the problem, she explained. The product was both reliable and cheap and seemed outdated, especially when compared with the elegantly packaged cosmetics of Helena Rubinstein and Elizabeth Arden.

A few years earlier, Resor had successfully used sex appeal to boost the sales of Woodbury soap. She had a new idea for Pond's. She

helen Lansdowne Resor understood that many women aspired "upward to the habits of richer people." And so, instead of sex appeal, she used class connotations to sell Pond's.

understood that many women aspired "upward to the habits of richer people." And so, instead of sex appeal, she used class connotations to sell Pond's. Resor's campaign featured women from high society explaining why they used the cosmetic. Alva Belmont was the first woman to appear in the campaign.

Alva Belmont was not a diva, a flapper, or a new American woman. She wasn't even young. She was, however, a wealthy socialite and very famous. She was the wife of William Vanderbilt, one of the richest men in the United States. To convince Alva Belmont to provide "testimony" for Pond's, Resor struck a deal. Pond's would make a one-thousand-dollar donation to the National Woman's Party, an organization Belmont supported. In exchange, the society leader agreed to speak on behalf of Pond's Cold Cream. She had one demand. She refused to allow her photograph to appear in the advertisement. That would be just a little too common for someone of her social standing.

Resor agreed. The advertisement showed a photograph of Alva Belmont's library, a rather odd choice but still one that would interest women. It gave them the impression of being inside the Belmont mansion. The text, however, is what sold the product. The copy read like a magazine interview:

> *"Just how important do you think personal appearance is?" the interviewer asked.*
>
> *"It is vital," Alva Belmont answered. "This is just as true for the woman at home or in business as for those who are socially prominent."*
>
> *She continued, "A person may have great intelligence and yet make a very bad impression if her appearance is careless. So we do ourselves a great injustice if we do not give our bodies great care. It is very wise in every way to cultivate the knowledge of how to keep ourselves presentable and young."*

Not until well into the interview did Belmont make the plug for Pond's: "That why I advise the daily use of Pond's Two

What one of Society's twelve most beautiful women says about the care of the skin

PORTRAIT BY NEYSA MCMEIN

MRS. BIDDLE DUKE

"The woman who achieves loveliness must be exquisite at all times. Her skin should be so perfectly cared for that every situation finds it the same—smooth and transparently clear—unlined by fatigue, showing no trace of exposure. And this I believe any woman can accomplish with the careful use of Pond's Two Creams."

Cordelia Biddle Duke

Or course if one did nothing but recline upon a chaise longue in a foam of Venise lace and chiffon, such terms as fatigue and exposure would be unknown.

But the woman who is active in society leads a very different sort of life.

The younger ones (to say nothing of their mothers and aunts) are almost invariably enthusiastic sportswomen. Indeed their strenuous daytime programme of skating, riding, or golf only serves to inspire their slim silver sandals right through until four o'clock the next morning.

But sports and late hours combine in an insidious attack upon woman's dearest possession—her complexion.

The icy wind that sweeps across the frozen pond is leaving tiny cracks and roughnesses. The merciless sun of seasides is bound to burn and coarsen. The laughing hours of post-midnight dancing will show next morning in faint lines of fatigue around eyes and mouth.

But—"exquisite at all times" is the society woman's code, as Mrs. Biddle Duke says. And exquisite at all times she is.

Long ago the women who led an active social life discovered a sure and simple method of skin care that actually frees the skin from the injuries their strenuous life would cause—keeps it at all times as clear and fresh and delicate as their position has always demanded.

This method is the famous one devised by Pond's. After years of study and research, the Pond's chemists pronounced the two skin essentials for every woman to be—Cleansing and Protection. And to this end they worked and experimented until Pond's Cold Cream and Pond's Vanishing Cream were produced.

Exquisite women use this Method

Pond's Cold Cream for cleansing is a deliciously soft pure cream that not only cleanses the skin thoroughly, but restores its natural satin suppleness. Dip your fingers into its fragrant softness and rub an ample amount on your face and neck. The fine oil in it sinks deep into the pores to dislodge all of the dirt, excess natural oil, and powder that invisibly clog those tiny cells. Now wipe it off with a soft cloth and don't be ashamed if the cloth is black. *Do this twice.* How clean your skin is, how soft and velvety and above all how fine! That is because the tiny pores now have a chance to breathe and function normally.

Pond's Vanishing Cream is now smoothed on. This light delicate cream is used after every skin cleansing, leaving a new fresh loveliness that prepares your skin perfectly for the necessary finish of powder.

As Miss Cordelia Biddle of Philadelphia, young Mrs. Duke began her social life against the brilliant background of one of America's most exclusive families. She is one of the most prominent and most admired of the younger women of society and is well-known on both sides of the Atlantic. Her captivating personality is coupled with a beauty that made Neysa McMein, well-known

artist and illustrator, whose charming portrait of Mrs. Duke is shown above, choose her as one of the twelve most beautiful women in America.

TODAY, ALL WOMEN WHO MUST BE EXQUISITE HAVE A NEW CONCEPTION OF SKIN CARE. ITS FOUNDATION IS POND'S TWO CREAMS—ONE FOR THE NEW REJUVENATING CLEANSING, ONE FOR THE DELICATE PROTECTIVE FINISH THAT FOLLOWS . . . . . .
EVERY SKIN NEEDS THESE TWO CREAMS

Smooth on only a little. There's a new glow to your whole face—and how extraordinarily young you're looking! The powder will go on more smoothly than ever and will last almost indefinitely.

Together these two creams provide the balanced treatment that every skin requires. Pond's Cold Cream effects a deep purifying of the skin that a mere surface cleansing can never accomplish. And immaculate Pond's cleanliness is the sure prevention and cure for such distressing blemishes as a lifeless muddy skin and over-active oil glands that result in the bane of all women—a shiny nose.

Pond's Vanishing Cream actually protects the skin from the constant attacks of every-day life that are so hard to realize. Fine lines and wrinkles that every woman dreads, chapping and roughplaces are the result of simply every-day exposure. Wind that dries and roughens, sun that burns and coarsens are to be met with whenever one goes out of the house. But the woman who cares about her skin can laugh at these ever-present foes, for she knows that her complexion protected as it is by Pond's Two Creams, has nothing to fear from them.

When to use it

Every night give your face and neck a thorough cleansing with Pond's Cold Cream. If your skin is inclined to be dry, put a little more cream on for the night and let the skin absorb naturally the oils it lacks. And by all means rub a little into the point of your elbow if you want a soft round accent to your arm instead of the dreadful turkey look that so many elbows have.

In the morning freshen your face with water—Pond's Cold Cream, again, if your skin is dry—then apply Pond's Vanishing Cream for a delicious texture and perfect powder base. Powder and, if you wish, a trace of rouge. This cream should be used just as often as you cleanse your face.

After a long motor ride, a dusty journey by train, a windy afternoon of golf, be sure to use Pond's Cold Cream as you come in, following it, of course, with Pond's Vanishing Cream before powdering.

If you are entertaining or going out in the evening use Pond's Cold Cream followed by Pond's Vanishing Cream for smooth clear loveliness.

Remember, the transparent clearness for which the fashionable woman is distinguished is the result of daily care. Begin this method at once and you will see the same loveliness reflected in your own mirror. Pond's Two Creams may be had at all drug and department stores. The Pond's Extract Company.

FREE OFFER

Mail this coupon at once and we will send you, free, tubes of these two famous creams that usually sell for ten cents each.

Speaking for Pond's Cold Cream in this ad that ran in McCall's magazine in 1924, socialite Cordelia Biddle Duke talks of how hard the life of a socialite is on a woman's complexion—"their strenuous daytime programme of skating, riding, or golf only inspires their slim silver sandals right through until four o'clock the next morning . . . but 'exquisite at all times' is the society woman's code. . . ."

Creams, so that women can keep their charm and influence as long as they need them—and that is always."

Helen Resor had done it again. The advertisement was tasteful. It didn't look like an advertisement at all but rather like a magazine article. Women's interest in the lives of socialites ensured they would read the interview. The real success, however, was Alva Belmont's endorsement of the product. If a woman as intelligent, charming, and wealthy as Belmont would use Pond's, then the product must be good.

The campaign was so successful that a string of additional testimonials for Pond's featuring other society matrons appeared in popular magazines. Unlike Alva Belmont, each of these elegant women agreed to be photographed. Vanderbilt, Morgan, Drexel, and Du Pont—these were the names of the wealthiest families in the United States. One would never dare to accuse *them* of being soap-and-water women.

These African American women exhibit the best of flapper fashion in New York's Harlem neighborhood in 1927.

Charm and the colored girl beautiful

In 1920 James Weldon Johnson wrote an article titled "Beautiful Women" that appeared in the *New York Age*. He was an African American poet and journalist, a former ambassador to Venezuela, and a leader in the National Association for the Advancement of Colored People (NAACP). In his article, he poetically described beautiful white women. At least one African American woman took offense at his words. She picked up her pen and wrote an editorial of her own for the *Cleveland Advocate*. "We are somewhat surprised," she wrote, "that Mr. Johnson . . . did not include our Colored women and provide a place for them among his beautiful women." She pressed her point:

> *. . . where dwells woman more beautiful than our Colored women?*
>
> *Among them we have the Castilian [from a region in Spain] type: rich, creamy complexions, hair as black as the features on the raven, eyes that are "deep wells of mystery." . . . we have them with complexions as fair as the lily when it opens its full bloom on Easter morn, and with golden tresses of angelic beauty or nut-brown in color; we have them, veritable Cleopatras [dark-skinned Egyptian queen of first century B.C.], with the most fascinating high-brown complexions and lips as red as the first ripe strawberry when the morning's dew bathes it; and last but not least, we have them, too, complexioned with deep, fadeless, reverential black.*

Although she could have passed for white, soprano Madame Hackley made it a point to ride in segregated railroad cars as she traveled the South raising funds for African American classical musicians.

Beauty means different things to different people. For African American women and men, society's concept of beauty was a complicated subject and one that often smacked of white supremacy. What was beautiful to the white community was not necessarily beautiful to people of color. Middle- and upper-class white society dominated the beauty industry in the 1920s and 1930s. The African American community, however, was not about to accept those beauty standards as their own.

Madame E. Azalia Hackley, a well-known concert soprano, was a "race woman," as many African Americans referred to themselves. In

1916 she published a book called *The Colored Girl Beautiful*. In the foreword, she explained how she had come to write the book. She had been visiting with the dean of the girls' department at Tuskegee Institute in Alabama. The school was one of the largest African American colleges in the country. The dean asked Hackley to speak to the women students. "What shall I talk about?" Hackley asked.

"Tell them anything you think they should know. They will believe an experienced woman like you who travels and knows the world and life," replied the dean.

And so she began a talk full of statements that smack of racism to the modern reader:

"Beauty is a matter of personal opinion. To a savage African, a baby with a black skin and flat nose is the ideal.

"To a Chinese, a lump, yellow, slant-eyed baby . . .

"To the Esquimaux [Eskimo], the round faced, small eyed, black haired little baby . . .

"A child should be taught to love and be proud of its race and to know the good points of the race."

Although her statements sound racist,

"A child should be taught to love and be proud of its race and to know the good points of the race."

—Madame Hackley, 1916

A few minutes later, the diva of opera stood alone before "a sea of colored faces" staring up at her. Hackley was no stranger to an audience, and yet she felt overwhelmed. She asked, "May I sit down, girls?"

"Would you like to talk about Love— real Love?" she asked.

"Yes, yes," came the answer.

"Would you like to talk about Beauty— real Beauty?"

"Yes! Yes!" they answered and the chairs were pulled forward.

Hackley was actually very forward thinking for her time. She gave many talks to more audiences of young women, and eventually, she collected her talks into a book. Its message lived long after Hackley died: Beauty was accepting yourself for the person you were and not imitating a media representation. Love and beauty could not be separated. Nor could they be found in the pages of a magazine or jar of cold cream or a tube of mascara, for they did not reside in those things. Real love and real beauty grew from deep inside each person.

Chapter Five

The Backlash against Modern Times

Forbade His Wife to Become 'Modern'
So Mrs. James C. Ellington Sues for Divorce from Her Chicago Husband

—Headline in *New York Times*, August 18, 1923

Mid-1920s cartoon by Bertram Prance

Throughout the 1920s,

churches spoke out against the bare legs and wild behavior of what the media was calling flaming youth. But young people didn't seem to care.

Prohibition was the law. Still, public drunkenness was an ugly problem. Worse, speakeasies had sprouted like mushrooms in the city. These secret private clubs sold bootleg (illegal) liquor. The owners cleverly disguised them. One might enter through the back doors of a florist's shop or a funeral home or even through a phony telephone booth right on Broadway in New York City. With a knock on the door and a whispered password, a man or woman could enter. All night long, they sang, danced, and drank, laughing in the face of the law. Before Prohibition, said one modern lady, "no decent woman could go into a bar, but now nobody is surprised at our being there."

Women had won the right to vote. Still, they wanted more—equal rights in pay and employment opportunities. Some radical women were even organizing planned parenthood clinics where they might teach poor immigrant women how to prevent unwanted pregnancies. Other radical women—or

Social activist Lucia Ames Mead (above) *worked closely with Jane Addams in speaking out against the evils of war.*

female activists, such as Lucia Ames Mead, were traveling the country and speaking at schools against war and the U.S. military. Some accused these women of planting seeds of lawlessness in the minds of youth.

Modern times were shaking up the United States. Those who feared the social changes of the 1920s looked around for someone or something to blame. For some, the culprits were the Catholics who had infiltrated the police forces in many U.S. cities. Some Protestants feared that Catholic teachers in public school were brainwashing their children in the beliefs of the Roman Catholic Church. Others blamed African Americans who were moving into white neighborhoods, arguing their right to live wherever they pleased. Some characterized the music performed by black musicians— jazz, ragtime, and blues—as "primitive" and indecent. Still others blamed the Jewish populations. People made sweeping generalizations claiming that Jews owned all U.S. businesses and controlled Hollywood. And Hollywood, in turn, was to blame because the silver screen teased youth with images of loose women and likable gangsters.

In the eyes of some outraged Americans, foreigners and radical women were stealing their country. Something had to be done.

Women
of the Klan

In 1923 an advertisement circulated throughout Seattle, Washington. It called upon women to join a new organization, one that claimed to support American ideals and patriotism. "To the American Women of Washington," it began:

Are you interested in the welfare of our Nation?. . . Are you interested in Better Government? Do you not wish for the protection of Pure Womanhood? Shall we uphold the sanctity of the American Home? Should we not interest ourselves in Better Education for our children? Do we not want American teachers in our American schools? It is possible for organized patriotic women to aid in stamping out the crime and vice that are undermining the morals of our youth.

Many women were members of the Ku Klux Klan (above), *an organization that violently promoted white supremacy.*

Halfway across the country, in Indiana, a similar advertisement called upon women, whether a housewife or a career woman, "to put her splendid efforts and abilities behind a movement for 100 percent American women." The organization was the Women's Ku Klux Klan (WKKK).

The history of the Ku Klux Klan dates to 1866 and Reconstruction (1865–1877). During this period after the Civil War, African Americans had newly won rights, including the right to own property, run for political office, and vote. These rights represented a great deal of progress for African Americans (although the rights to run for office and to vote extended only to men). But not everyone supported African American rights. Many southern states passed Jim Crow laws, which were designed to keep blacks and whites apart.

Although Jim Crow laws varied from state to state, overall the result was much the same: Black people's lives were severely restricted. A black child could not attend the same school as a white child. A black woman could not shop in the same stores as a white woman. Health care and employment opportunities were also limited.

Jim Crow laws had been well entrenched in the southern United States since the end of the Civil War. This photograph shows a barrier requiring black passengers to sit in the rear section of a bus.

Most black people followed Jim Crow laws. They created their own neighborhoods. They opened groceries, funeral parlors, churches, and schools. But bigotry extended beyond the law books. If an African American showed any disrespect to a white person, the African American might become the victim of violence. Disrespect might be something as simple as not lowering eyes in the presence of a white person or not stepping aside to let a white person pass. Should a black man or woman be accused of a crime, angry mobs often stormed the jailhouse and lynched (hung) the offender before any trial got under way.

The Ku Klux Klan began in these years following the Civil War with the goal of enforcing Jim Crow laws and upholding what it called "racial purity." Only men could join, and each sealed his membership with a sworn oath to uphold the racist beliefs of the organization. Within a decade, however, pressure from the U.S. government caused many chapters of the KKK to disband. And yet Jim Crow laws and racial violence continued. The National Association for the Advancement of Colored People formed as a way for African Americans to fight discrimination and to overturn Jim Crow laws.

Before the Great War, most African Americans lived in southern states. During and after the war, industry in northern cities expanded. African Americans moved to the North, hoping to find jobs and better lives. Soon a great migration began as hundreds of thousands of blacks left their rural shacks and headed for cities such as Saint Louis, Chicago, and Cleveland. "It was not as easy for women as it was for men to hop freight trains and if money was saved for tickets it was men who were usually sent," said historian Hazel V. Carby. Even so, women, too, found ways to escape the poverty of the South for new lives in the North.

Many white men and women believed that modern times were evil, and they joined KKK chapters as a way to reform society.

As more and more African Americans crowded into northern cities, they settled in neighborhoods that had previously been all white. Racial tension increased. Although there were no Jim Crow laws there, these migrants faced many of the same restrictions they

Citizens are shown lining up to vote in 1926. The influx of blacks into New York City formed the basis for the Harlem Renaissance—an artistic and intellectual movement that created a new black cultural identity. Novelist Zora Neale Hurston, singer Josephine Baker, and poet Gwendolyn Brooks were among the African American women who were part of this movement.

had experienced in the South. Many hospitals did not treat black patients. Many schools did not welcome black children. For women, domestic work as maids, cooks, or washerwomen was often the best chance they had for earning a living. Employers denied black men membership in labor unions and so they, too, were shut out of better-paying jobs.

During this period, the Ku Klux Klan resurfaced. The revival was due in part to the changes of modern times—the flapper's flashy rebellion and the outright disregard for Prohibition laws. Many men and women believed that modern times were evil, and they joined KKK chapters as a way to reform society. But many more joined the KKK as a reaction to the migration of blacks to northern cities and the continued demand for equality

of the races. As a result, KKK chapters formed in northern states, including Illinois, Ohio, Pennsylvania, and Massachusetts.

Flappers, bootleggers, and African Americans were not the sole focus of KKK hatred or violence. Immigration to the United States was at an all-time high in the early decades of the twentieth century, and immigrants were targets as well. There was no place for "foreigners" in the modern-day KKK's philosophy of One Hundred Percent Americanism.

In the 1800s, the KKK was limited to men. In 1921 the Imperial Wizard (leader) of the KKK announced that the organization had voted to admit women as members. The time had come, he said, "to give women recognition." Why did the KKK have a sudden change of heart about women?

A Nickel, a Prayer,
and a Woman's Responsibility

Just as white women were called to action in the 1920s, so, too, were African American women. They wanted the same things that other women wanted: good schools and churches and opportunities for employment. "Women want homes in which purity can be taught, not homes that are police court feeders," wrote Arnetta Hill in the *Ohio Monitor,* an African American publication. "They want the pool rooms closed and the gambling dens of every variety swept out of existence."

Their call to action, however, differed from the WKKK's. Rather than target another race for harassment, they urged their black sisters to uplift their own race. "Young women, did it ever occur to you that you have a great and awful responsibility resting upon you, and that you in part hold destiny of our race in your hands?" wrote Arnetta Hill. "It has been said, 'Whatever the women are, the men will sure to be' . . . the power is yours. . . . It belongs to you as a woman."

Jane Edna Hunter was one young woman who answered the call to African American women long before Arnetta Hill wrote her newspaper editorial. Jane's parents were poor farmers in South Carolina. By the age of ten, Jane was working as a household helper, washing and ironing for a white employer.

Jane Edna Hunter offered young southern black women training and guidance and a place to live while they looked for work in the North. Her Cleveland, Ohio, facility became a model for similar projects across the United States.

The employer, however, taught Jane to read and write. Jane took that little bit of education and promise and pulled herself up. At eighteen she had completed an eighth-grade education, more than most girls—but she wanted more in her life. She enrolled in the Hampton Institute, a vocational school in Hampton, Virginia, where she earned a nursing degree. And still she wanted more.

In 1905 Hunter left Virginia for Cleveland, Ohio, armed with only "a nickel and a prayer," as she put it. Although Jim Crow laws did not rule this northern city, Hunter still faced discrimination. She was a double minority—black and female. In time, however, she put her education and her ambition to work. Then she turned her energy to helping the hundreds of African American women who were fleeing the South for a brighter life in northern cities, just as she had done years earlier.

With other African American women, she founded the Working Girls Association. She opened a settlement house (an institution for social services) with more than twenty rooms. For those young women who found a temporary home there, it was "a dream come true." The home provided more than shelter. It gave the women the means to become self-sufficient. It offered vocational training in beauty, music, and secretarial work as well as club activities. There was even a kindergarten to educate the children of single mothers.

The *Cleveland Advocate,* a newspaper published by and for the African American community, sang Hunter's praises. "South Carolina may preserve the memory of her Henrys, Calhouns and Pickens," wrote Ralph W. Tyler in 1919 about the white male heroes of that state, "but greater than these is the Colored woman—Jane Hunter—who, although born in obscurity, nursed in poverty, and nourished on oppression down in South Carolina, made an oasis in a desert."

Jane Hunter was thirty-seven when Ralph Tyler wrote about her achievements. And still, Hunter wanted more. She continued her education, earning a law degree in 1925 from the Baldwin-Wallace College in Ohio. Her home for girls in need also grew. The home moved to a much larger building with eighty apartments. Thousands of young black women passed through its doors. It eventually became the Phillis Wheatley Association. (Wheatley was a slave from Africa who became educated and eventually published a book of her poetry. She was set free in the late 1700s.)

In the early decades of the twentieth century, many social organizations such as the Young Women's Christian Association (YWCA) were segregated. The YWCA barred women of color from membership. Some African Americans objected to Hunter's organization for the same reason. Being intended for African American females, it was likewise segregated. They would have preferred that women of color be treated equally but not separately. Hunter, however, remained committed to helping young girls of her race.

Perhaps the passage of the Nineteenth Amendment, giving women the right to vote in state and national elections, was one reason. Women who were members of the WKKK might be more inclined to vote into public office those people who shared the organization's racist beliefs.

The women's chapters of the Ku Klux Klan were separate from the men's. Their racial hatred and intolerance of Catholic and Jewish religions, however, burned just as violently as the men's. The WKKK creed rested on this essential point: the American home and American womanhood was the foundation upon which rested the future of the United States. But not all women were "100 percent American," they believed. Only those who were white, Protestant, and born in the United States were truly Americans. The WKKK pamphlets describe these Americans as "the salt of the Earth." Immigrants, however, were described as the "refuse populations of other lands." Refuse was another word for "that which is rotten and discarded."

Millions of women joined the movement in the 1920s. Some were the wives and daughters of Klansmen, who joined to support their men. However, historian Kathleen Blee points out that many women joined the WKKK first and then encouraged their husbands to join the Klan as well. By the mid-1920s, approximately two million men and women were members of KKK chapters.

Like Klansmen, the Klanswomen attended rallies and wore white hooded robes, often embroidered with a large cross on the breast. "What a thrill when we were told to assemble at a certain place wearing our robes, then marching with others also unknown to us," wrote one member of a WKKK chapter in Indiana. She joined the organization after a WKKK leader had told her that it was an organization of "better known and educated women" who supported "100% Americanism."

Like Klansmen, the women burned crosses and gave speeches on the need to keep the white race pure. Ensuring "racial purity" meant much more than segregating whites from blacks. It meant voting

> **"Well may the Colored citizen now prepare for serious trouble,"** stated one article. **"Wise Colored people will make all legal preparations for protection at once."**

—quote from an article in the *Cleveland Union*, 1921

KKK politicians into office. It meant opposing the hiring and encouraging the firing of Catholic and Irish schoolteachers. It meant boycotting Jewish-owned businesses. Daisy Barr of the WKKK in Indiana spoke rabidly against Jewish store owners. "Jews had 75 percent of the money in the United States." She warned, "The WKKK would shut down every Jewish business in Indianapolis."

It also meant closing the doors to the many thousands of immigrants who arrived in the United States each year. The Klan felt that the slums where these immigrants lived were a "breeding place of the moron . . . and criminal."

African American communities responded to the formation of the WKKK with warnings published in their newspapers. "Well may the Colored citizen now prepare for serious trouble," stated one article. "The female of the species is more deadly than the male. . . . Wise Colored people will make all legal preparations for protection at once."

Equal Rights
for Women

In 1920 Congress had passed the Nineteenth Amendment, but it was a bitter pill for some male politicians to swallow. Many did not believe that women were smart enough to understand politics or to vote in an informed way. Others simply feared that the millions of new voters—women all—might vote them out of office!

For a woman to vote, she first had to register. Newspapers reported that in some southern states, such as North Carolina, Tennessee, Mississippi, and Florida, workers in registration offices had quit their jobs rather than register women voters. In the autumn of 1920, a number of black women walked into the Jefferson County courthouse in Birmingham, Alabama, intending to vote. According to an article in the *Cleveland Advocate*, they were told, "The state of Alabama doesn't want you."

Turning away someone who wished to

register to vote simply because that person was a woman or, more often, an African American woman was illegal. Women had won the right to vote, but all women, no matter their race, were still a minority in the political arena. Even as late at 1928, laws still discriminated against women in many states.

In Oklahoma, for example, the law stated that a woman could not run for any of the major offices in state government. Wisconsin's state law prohibited a woman from running for governor. In more than half the states, women could not serve on a jury during a court trial.

In six states, property laws still gave a husband the right to take his wife's wages. In eight states, a wife's share of the property—the house, the furnishings, and her clothing—remained under her husband's control for as long as he lived. In Pennsylvania a husband could divorce his wife if doctors had determined she was a "lunatic,"—in other words, mentally ill. A woman, however, could not divorce her husband on the basis of mental illness.

A Michigan state law prohibited women from working at a job that might be hazardous to her health or to her morals. Men, however, could work at whatever job they could get, no matter the risks to their lives or morals. Ohio, also, prohibited women from holding specific jobs such as driving a taxi or handling baggage or freight. Nor could women work in Ohio's pool halls, bowling alleys, or shoe-shining parlors. Most likely, the reason for this law was

Eleanor Roosevelt (back row, middle) *felt that it was important for women to work together as a group. She was an active participant in women's organizations for all of her adult life. She is shown here in 1923 with a group working toward educating people about democracy.*

that mostly men—and often rough men at that—frequented these places and were thought to negatively influence women's behavior.

Eleanor Roosevelt was an outspoken supporter of woman's rights. In 1928 her husband, Franklin D. Roosevelt, was the governor of New York. That year she wrote an article for *Redbook* magazine, expressing her disappointment in women's inability to obtain any of the political power that rested in the hands of men. She wrote:

> Women have been voting for ten years. But have they achieved actual political equality with men? No. . . . In small things they are listened to; but when it comes to asking for important things they generally find they are up against a blank wall. . . . The machinery of party politics has always been in the hands of men, and still is.

The machinery of party politics has always been in the hands of men, and still is.

—Eleanor Roosevelt, 1928

How could women get their fair share of political power? Some women believed that they should form a political party of their own, rather than joining the political parties to which men belonged. Eleanor Roosevelt had a different idea. Women must learn to play the same political games that men played, she said. Men supported one another. Women, likewise, had to nominate, support, and vote women into public offices. Once they held positions in city and state governments, they could begin to alter the state laws.

Having more women serving on city councils and in state government sounded like a simple solution. But it wasn't. Society, in general, still believed that a woman's first responsibility was to her family, not her community or her country. Men could handle those important issues. A writer for the *New York Times* praised Eleanor Roosevelt for her outspoken belief in woman's rights. But the newspaper made a point to emphasize that Roosevelt was first and foremost the wife of the governor and mother to his children. The reporter wrote, "She believes that a woman fitted to serve her community or her country can show that fitness best in the management of her own home. . . ."

Roosevelt did believe that. But she also believed women should enter the public sphere. She encouraged them to study history, business, and political methods. She urged women to leave their homes and volunteer in any number of community and social projects that might make their country a better place in which to live. Women could not rely on men to speak for them. They had to learn how to speak for themselves.

For a time, it seemed as if women had found a unified voice. In the early 1920s, hundreds of thousands of infants died each year from poor nutrition and unsanitary conditions. Women joined together to pressure Congress to do something about this. They supported the passage of the Sheppard-Towner bill. This bill would provide funding to establish community health clinics and to train mothers in how to care for their infants. "Mothers will do better when they know better," the women argued. Some members of Congress protested. Government had no business, they said, entering the homes of women and telling them how to care for their children. Even so, Congress passed the bill by an overwhelming margin.

This 1921 photograph shows a miner's daughter holding her younger sibling. The Sheppard-Towner bill established the idea of providing government help for poor children.

But experience had shown that political winds never blow with the same strength or even in the same direction for long. By the mid-1920s, elected officials began to realize that many women did not go to the polls to vote. Furthermore, male politicians realized that not all women thought alike. Race, social class, religion, education, and family experiences shaped their beliefs. That, in turn, shaped the way they voted—when they voted.

Emily Newell Blair was a middle-class housewife who entered public life soon after the passage of the Nineteenth Amendment. In the 1920s, she became the vice-chair of the Democratic National

Committee. Hers was a power-ful position. But even Blair admitted that women's politi-cal influence by the mid-1920s had become more of a tap than a punch. "I know of no woman today who has any influence or political power because she is a woman," she said. "I know of no woman who has a following of other women. I know of no politician who is afraid of the woman vote on any question under the sun."

Without political power, a group's social concerns will not draw the attention or the sup-port of those who make laws.

Emily Newell Blair

Alice Paul

ment that stated: "Men and women shall have equal rights throughout the United States and every place subject to its jurisdiction." Those who sup-ported the bill saw it as a way to ensure equal wages and equal property laws for women. Women, like men, would serve on juries in all states. In all states, women's wages would be their own and not their hus-bands'. Even in Pennsylvania, the ERA would grant a wife the right to divorce her men-tally disturbed husband.

But not all women sup-ported the ERA. Those who opposed the amendment thought it might harm women. Laws had been passed earlier in the century to establish a minimum wage for a female worker and to limit the number of hours an employer might force her to work. The ERA could erase those beneficial gains, they feared. Another reason that some women opposed the amendment involved the issue of military service. Soon after the United States entered the Great War, Congress passed the Selective Service Act. This act gave the gov-ernment the right to draft men into the army. If women were equal to men, then couldn't they, too, be drafted into military service

Some male members of Congress must have sighed in relief when they perceived that although women had the right to vote, they were by and large disorganized and disinter-ested. Women's issues were not as urgent as they had been even just a few years earlier. By 1929 Congress had repealed the Sheppard-Towner Act, ending funding for children and maternal health education.

The failure of Congress to pass the Equal Rights Amendment (ERA) was also a backlash against modern times and the new American woman. Alice Paul of the National Woman's Party drafted the amend-

during a war? Many women as well as men shuddered at the thought!

Each year, as the new Congress met in Washington, D.C., politically active women pushed for the ERA. Other women who were equally passionate about politics pushed to block the ERA. Each year, Congress failed to pass it into law.

"Me for 'Ma'"

When Miriam A. Ferguson ran for governor of Texas in 1924, she made few political speeches. When she did speak in public, she read a few sentences in a quiet voice from a prepared sheet. She told the voters of Texas that she knew very little about state affairs. Politics was her husband's interest, not hers. If elected, she promised to follow the guidance of her husband. Her husband, James Ferguson, was a former governor of Texas who had been impeached for mishandling funds. Texas law prohibited him from running again for governor. And so, his wife ran instead.

Texans called her Ma, because of her initials. The Fergusons had stated that a vote for Ma was also a vote for Pa, her husband, giving the

Miriam A. Ferguson ran for governor of Texas, promising that a vote for her was a vote for her husband too.

state two governors for the price of one.

Women had won the right to vote just five years earlier. Should she win election, Ma Ferguson would become the first woman governor of Texas. One of her campaign slogans was a simple play with words: Me for Ma. Those who opposed her candidacy countered with: No Ma for Me—Too Much Pa.

Texans voted her into office. Feminists, however, were not impressed. Ma Ferguson had never been a suffragist, a woman who fought for women's rights, including the right to vote. After meeting with Governor Ferguson, some Texas feminists complained that the governor was a figurehead only, ruled by her husband. She did not have an opinion that was her own, they argued. Or if she did, she didn't express it. At least one feminist stated that she felt sorry for Ma, because her husband had forced her into politics.

Governor Ma Ferguson avoided the media spotlight whenever possible. A newspaper profile of her soon after her election stated that her greatest pride was managing her home. Even as governor, she spent hours each morning overseeing her household responsibilities, including caring for her chickens.

Governor Ross

Ma Ferguson was not the United States' first female state governor. That distinction went to Nellie Tayloe Ross of Wyoming.

Nellie Tayloe had been a kindergarten teacher when she married attorney William Bradford Ross. Ross had a successful law practice in Cheyenne and in 1922 won the election for governor. Less than two years later, however, he died. The state held a special election for a new governor, and the Democratic Party nominated Ross's wife for the office. Although Nellie Ross accepted the nomination, like Ma Ferguson, she did little campaigning. She wrote letters stating that she would enforce Prohibition laws. The voters of Wyoming voted Ross into office, largely as a tribute to her dead husband. Some voters cast their ballot for Ross so that Wyoming would become the first state to elect a woman governor.

The elections for governor in both Wyoming and Texas were held on the same day, and both women candidates won. Nellie Ross, however, took the oath of office fifteen days before Ma Ferguson, thus become the first female governor in the United States.

Although Ross held office in faraway Wyoming, the *New York Times* occasionally featured Governor Ross in its newspaper on the East Coast. In January 1925, the newspaper reported on the governor's speech to the state assembly. How the governor dressed for the occasion was apparently thought to be more newsworthy than what she said during her forty-five-minute speech. The headline read: "Mrs. Ross Wears Hat Before Legislature." The lead paragraph emphasized that no previous governor had ever worn a hat or gloves while addressing the assembly.

Nellie Ross was narrowly defeated for re-election as governor of Wyoming in 1926. President Franklin Roosevelt later appointed her the first female director of the U.S. Mint in 1933, a post she held for twenty years.

Women Make News in 1926:
The Strange Disappearance of Sister Aimee

In the 1920s, Aimee Semple McPherson was the most famous female evangelical preacher (advocating literal interpretation of the Bible and seeking others to do the same) in the United States. She was also one of the most controversial religious personalities of the decade. Many devoted followers believed McPherson was a messenger of God, sent to Earth to wash away the sins of modern times, such as drinking and gambling. On the other hand, many thought she was a phony, a Hollywood celebrity who staged elaborate variety shows in place of solemn religious ceremonies. (She once rode a motorcycle down the aisle of her temple in Los Angeles.)

Whether heavenly messenger or media personality, McPherson knew how to get attention. She was a master of the modern media. She understood the power of radio to reach hundreds of thousands of people. She purchased her own radio station to broadcast her sermons. Publicity won her new converts and helped to build her network of churches. The collection plate that circulated at each service returned to her full of paper money, not coins.

In May 1926, McPherson generated her most dramatic headlines of all—she disappeared. No one could prove McPherson's disappearance was a publicity stunt. But the police found her story—especially her escape through the desert—a little hard to believe. According to the newspapers, she had been swimming at Venice Beach in California. Her flock of followers feared she had drowned. Hundreds of men and women held a vigil on the beach. "She can't be dead," they sobbed. "She was too noble. Her work was too great."

They prayed for a miracle. Days passed, then weeks. And then a miracle really did seem to occur. McPherson reappeared! She told the excited news reporters who crowded around her a fantastic story: A young husband and wife had approached her on the beach, asking her to pray for their sick child. Once she was alone with them, however, McPherson realized that the couple had bad intentions. They drugged her and kidnapped her, taking her to Mexico. They hoped to get a huge ransom for her release. After weeks, McPherson escaped and walked for thirteen hours through the desert to safety in the United States.

Women preachers were extremely rare in the 1920s. And women preachers like Aimee Semple McPherson, who wore makeup and flamboyant clothes, were unheard of. McPherson drew huge crowds on her tours throughout the United States and abroad. Here she is shown in 1928 preaching to a huge crowd at London's Albert Hall.

McPherson's story was intriguing, but the evidence didn't seem to support it. McPherson's skin wasn't weathered or sunburned. And her shoes showed no sign of the hike she'd said she'd made to get home. Nor could police find the shack she claimed had been her prison. The district attorney in California charged her with falsifying evidence and corrupting public morals. He later dropped the charges.

Where had McPherson gone? Newspapers speculated for months. One report claimed she had run away with a secret lover to a seaside resort. McPherson stuck to her story, however, and her faithful followers stuck with her—at least for a few more years. By 1930 McPherson had lost her appeal, and her sensational sermons no longer made headlines.

Ma had brought the chickens to the state capital, Austin, from her farm. They scratched and clucked in the backyard of the governor's mansion. She generally arrived at her office in the state capital at about ten in the morning. Her husband, however, had arrived hours earlier. He sat in her office at a desk near hers. Ma disliked meeting with callers who came on state business. When she did, very often Pa was present and sometimes spoke for her. If someone proposed a policy or project Pa did not endorse, he might respond by suggesting that the governor, his wife, might not like that. One caller told reporters that Ma had been shelling pecans in the governor's office while James Ferguson was in the next room conducting state business. To the feminists' chagrin, Texas's first woman governor seemed to be a political puppet of her husband. She did not represent the liberated and independent new American woman.

Ma Ferguson ran for reelection in 1926 and lost. In 1932 she ran again and won. And again, Pa—not the governor—was in charge.

Caught in the Spider's Web

During the Great War, many women were pacifists, or people who oppose war. They joined peace movements. They did not want the United States to enter the war but rather attempt to solve international conflicts through discussion and mediation. Although their efforts failed, they continued to support mediation (diplomatic talks) even after the United States entered the war.

During the 1920s, peace organizations continued to draw members, especially women. The Women's International League for Peace and Freedom and the National Council for Prevention of War were two such organizations. Secretary of War John W. Weeks feared that these groups were undermining U.S. security, and so the U.S. government sometimes scrutinized them. Worse, rumors began circulating that the groups' members were Reds. *Red* was a slang word for "Communist." It was often used to describe those who questioned government. A Communist government had recently come to power in Russia, and many feared that Communists would try to take over the United States too.

In 1924 an important document begun to fuel the fears about peace activists. The document appeared in the *Dearborn Independent*, a newspaper printed by Henry Ford. Copies of the article soon circulated among politicians in the nation's capital. Known as "the spider-web chart," the document listed pacifist groups and the names of women who belonged to them. It accused the women of being part of a plot to overthrow the U.S. government.

The chart had been put together by a woman named Lucia R. Maxwell.

Women from all forty-eight states gathered in Washington, D.C., for a 1929 convention called the Fourth Conference on the Cause and Cure for War. Made up of nine national women's groups, the organization met every year until 1941, when the United States entered World War II (1939–1945).

The Raid

The police arrived at the brownstone house on West 18th Street in New York City without warning on an April morning in 1929. They had "stamped into the basement," said Margaret Sanger, and begun "tearing things to pieces." Mary Sullivan, who was the head of New York City's Policewomen's Bureau, led the raid on the Birth Control Clinical Research Bureau. Under her orders, the police locked the doors. The women patients who had come to the clinic that morning, some with infants, were not allowed to leave.

Margaret Sanger was a doctor and the founder of the clinic. She was no stranger to the police. Years earlier, she had been arrested for distributing information on birth control to women who requested it. But courts of law had granted doctors the right to provide such information to women patients. As the police squad began removing books from the shelves, Sanger demanded to see a search warrant. Mary Sullivan produced it, officially signed by a judge.

Margaret Sanger (third from the right) *joins other representatives at a 1925 conference of the American Birth Control League. At that time, the league, which would later become the Planned Parenthood Federation, had 27,500 members in chapters across the United States.*

When the police moved to the filing cabinets, again Dr. Sanger objected. "You have no right to touch those files," she said. "If you take them you will get into trouble."

The documents were the private records of the doctors who had examined patients. Mary Sullivan took them anyway. Her squad swept the papers from the tops of desks and even swept surgical instruments and rubber gloves into wastebaskets, all as potential evidence. A short time later, the police led the clinic's two doctors and three nurses—all women—into a paddy wagon (police van).

What law had these women broken? In 1929 Section 1142 of the New York State law prohibited anyone from communicating to any person information about contraceptives. However, another section of the law, 1145, allowed physicians to distribute contraceptives to women if the contraceptive might cure or prevent disease. Laws like these were common across the United States.

According to *Time* magazine, a police officer named Josephine McNamara had gone undercover to the clinic a few weeks earlier, posing as "the mother of three small children, the wife of a drunkard." The clinic doctors provided her with contraceptives. Three weeks later, that "evidence" led to the raid. McNamara participated in the raid. Margaret Sanger later learned that the judge had signed the search warrant without reading it.

The raid was a backlash against modern times. But the raid itself triggered still another backlash, this time from the medical community. A week later, the clinic's doctors and nurses appeared in court for a hearing. Seated in the courtroom were dozens of people—doctors, sociologists, and even a few clergymen. They had come in support of the accused women and the birth control clinic. The judge dismissed the case.

For the rest of her life, Margaret Sanger fought for the right of women to have access to birth control. The press frequently reminded its readers of Sanger's Irish heritage, attributing her fiery and fiesty spirit and stubborn courage as traits she inherited from her father. In time, the medical community came to accept the distribution of information about birth control to patients as an accepted practice. In time, too, society's attitudes toward contraception—and Margaret Sanger—would change, though slowly and not completely. Throughout the twentieth century, the controversy over birth control continued.

Maxwell was the librarian at the Chemical Warfare division of the War Department. On the chart, she listed more than those women who were pacifists. She accused most women's social organizations—including the Young Women's Christian Association, the National Council of Jewish Women, and the National League of Women Voters—of harboring Reds.

More than a backlash against modern times, the chart was slanderous. Suddenly, a Red Scare swept across the United States. Any woman—or man for that matter—who was a social reformer or a pacifist was eyed with suspicion. The women named on the chart, as well as many others, fought back.

Time magazine published an angry statement from Mrs. Clem L. Shaver, wife of the national campaign manager of the Democratic Party. She was not among those named on the chart, but she argued strongly that "all women are patriots . . . the women of America are not pacifists—they never have been."

"all women are patriots . . . the women of America are not pacifists—they never have been."

—Mrs. Clem L. Shaver, 1924

The members of the accused women's groups took their indignation and demands for an apology to John W. Weeks himself. In a letter to the secretary of war, dated April 2, 1924, Maud Wood Park, of the Women's Joint Congressional Committee (one of the organizations accused of harboring Reds), wrote:

> *My dear Mr. Secretary:*
> *I cannot understand why an employee of a government*
> *bureau should be permitted . . . to attack the women's*
> *organizations of the country and the women voters in these*

organizations. They wonder where the funds come from whereby these attacks are made.

These [words] are scurrilous [vulgar] and libelous and insulting to every woman voter in these women's organizations. We again protest in the strongest terms against the use of them in this connection. . . .

Twelve million women voters in these organizations do not propose to bear this scurrilous and contemptible attack by a subordinate in a government department without redress [remedy].

Carrie Chapman Catt, who had fought long and hard for the passage of the Nineteenth Amendment and women's rights, wrote articles in popular magazines. Women have been attacked, she protested, and without just cause. "Call us radical if you wish," Catt wrote, "but cease in charging us with conduct short of treason."

The secretary of war responded that the chart would be destroyed. Perhaps it was.

Carrie Chapman Catt turned her strong speaking and organizational skills to working for peace in the aftermath of World War I.

And yet, some people who had received copies of the chart kept them for reference. The damage had already been done. The reputation of women social reformers would suffer for many decades.

The End of the Roaring Twenties

The most dramatic backlash against modern times was not the outcry of the older generations against "flaming youth." It was not the violent attacks of the Ku Klux Klan or even the vicious rumors that women social reformers were plotting to overthrow the U.S. government. The event that would truly shake the United States to its knees was financial. On Monday, October 29, 1929, the stock market crashed.

A stock is a piece of paper. It represents a percentage of ownership in a company. That company may be an automobile manufacturer, a steel mill, or a factory. When the value of the company goes up, so does the value of its stock. The stockholders, or investors, make a profit. Throughout the 1920s, Americans were stock hungry. Even people who didn't have

Bad news of the stock market crash of 1929 filled the newspapers, as the decade of the Roaring Twenties came to an end. The 1930s would be a time of economic hardships, known as the Great Depression.

enough money to invest in stocks found a way to do so anyway. They borrowed from banks if they had to. Other Americans who didn't play the stock market gambled with money in another way. Banks and businesses made it possible for them to purchase things through a "buy now, pay later" plan. People borrowed money to purchase automobiles and homes. As long as they had a job, they could make their payments.

When the market crashed, the value of stocks fell dramatically until all those pieces of paper became worthless. Within days, businesses and the people who had invested in them lost everything.

The ripple effect of the crash spread outward across the United States. It continued spreading for years. Everyone suffered.

"Prosperity is more than economic condition; it is a state of mind," wrote historian Frederick Lewis Allen in *Only Yesterday*, a history of the 1920s. He likened the disastrous crash of the stock market in October and November 1929 to "a fall over Niagara." As hard times got worse, alarm and fear gripped the nation.

The Great Depression (1929–1942) had begun.

Change and continuity
and what comes next

*t*he economic depression has been and still is so extensive
that very few homes have escaped altogether
the anxieties that these last three years have brought.

—Grace Abbot, *New York Times*, 1922

(Above) *Migrant agricultural worker's family in Nipomo, California, photographed by Dorothea Lange, 1936*

In 1921 African American diva Ethel Waters

sang the blues about a man who had walked out on her. "From now on there'll be a change in me," she sings. She vows to change more than her appearance. She will change her attitude. She will not be hurt by love again.

The song came at the beginning of a decade when social change was sweeping the United States. In that era, Congress had passed two amendments to the U.S. Constitution—Prohibition and the right for women to vote. Industry and science took giant leaps forward, and as a result, transportation and communications changed. Relationships between mothers and daughters and husbands and wives also changed.

During these years, popular culture reflected not one but many images of the modern woman. She was a diva who appeared onstage and on the movie screen. She was a flapper who parked her corset in the restroom and danced in loose-fitting short skirts. She was the new American woman who voted for the first time ever, who graduated from college and started a career as well as a family. She was Mrs. Consumer, more scientifically aware than her mother had ever been. She was Miss Innocent, catlike and stalking a husband. She was also Mrs. Grundy, who grumbled about the immorality of modern times. And she was even a racist who wore a white hood and marched with a U.S. flag.

Taken together, these historical and cultural images created a composite character, a modern woman who could not be summarized by a single adjective or even a single sentence. She was not frail or delicate. She did not swoon or sob. She was thin or wanted to be. She wore cosmetics. She did not wear cosmetics. She went to the movies. She read books and wrote them too. Many of these modern girls and women asked themselves, "Who am I?" Some found answers in the advertisements that showed them how to dress and look younger or in the books that advised them on how to be truly beautiful no matter the color of your skin or the shape of your lips. Some found the answers by observing their own communities and taking action—opening health clinics, fighting for women's rights, or investigating untruthful advertisements and poisons in consumer products.

By the end of the decade, however, the mood of the United States was once again changing. The flapper fad ended. Women's skirts once again covered their knees and most of their legs. Advertisements would still appeal to women, but the persuasive language would shift from the frivolous to the practical. "Warm dependable coats for small budgets," read one advertisement from 1932, showing smiling women wrapped in their belted coats. The prices listed were $7.98 and $9.98. Movies would still lure audiences, but the themes of the stories would change to mirror the more difficult times of economic depression and another world war.

"Nothing about me is going to be the same," Ethel Waters sang. But that wasn't quite true, because some things did not change—important things such as the fight for justice and civil rights, the need most people have to belong, to be loved, to feel that their lives are meaningful. Those things are constant no matter the decade.

Although the 1930s and 1940s were going to be hard years for both men and women, neither the world nor the women would stand still. Amelia Earhart had volunteered as a nurse's aide during the Great War. In 1928 she became the first woman to fly a plane across the Atlantic Ocean. Her greatest achievements, however, were still ahead of her. During the 1920s, Mildred "Babe" Didrikson was a tomboy growing up in a Texas town, kicking and throwing a football as well as any boy. In the 1930s, she would turn U.S. athletics into a girl's game too.

In the 1920s, Marian Anderson rose above racial discrimination to become a diva of the opera stage. And yet the 1930s would bring her a dramatic opportunity to fight for justice—not just for herself but for

By the end of the 1920s, fashion and fun had turned to careful spending. What would the flapper have thought of these seventy-nine-cent poplin dresses offered in a Sears® catalog little more than a decade later?

her race. Eleanor Roosevelt would join hands with her. In the 1920s, she, too, had only begun to speak her mind.

Ah, but their stories—Earhart's, Didrikson's, Anderson's, and Roosevelt's—are the stuff of another decade. The story continues in *Rosie and Mrs. America: Perceptions of Women in the 1930s and 1940s.*

Source Notes

6 Frederick Lewis Allen, *Only Yesterday: An Informal History of the 1920s* (New York: Harper & Row, 1931), 68.

12 Ruth Hooper, "Flapping Not Repented Of," *New York Times*, July 16, 1922, BRM 7.

14 Sara Mayfield, *Exiles from Paradise: Zelda and Scott Fitzgerald* (New York: Delacorte Press, 1971), 20.

14 Ibid.

14 Margaret Mead, *Blackberry Winter: My Earlier Years* (New York: William Morrow & Co., 1972), 28.

14 Ibid.

15 Ibid.

16 Ibid., 87.

16 Ibid., 98.

17 Michael Immerso, *Coney Island: The People's Playground* (New Brunswick, NJ: Rutgers University Press, 2002), 127.

17 Ibid.

20 Frazier Hunt, "I Meet Miss Crawford," *Photoplay*, February 1934. Accessible at *Best of Everything: A Joan Crawford Encyclopedia*, n.d., http://www.joancrawfordbest.com/magphotoplay0234.htm (February 9, 2007).

20 Joan Cross, "Name Her and Win $1,000" in *Movie Weekly*, March 27, 1925. Accessible at *Best of Everything: A Joan Crawford Encyclopedia*, n.d. http://www.joancrawfordbest.com/magmoviewkly.htm (May 21, 2007).

20 "Mrs. Tone at Home" in *Life*, March 1, 1937. Accessible at *Best of Everything: A Joan Crawford Encyclopedia*, n.d., http://www.joancrawfordbest.com/articlelife37.htm (May 21, 2007).

22 *Time*, "Girl Under Moon," February 11, 1929, n.d., http://www.time.com/time/magazine/article/0,9171,737345,00.html, and Laura Muha, "Flash in the Sky," n.d., http://www.newsday.com/community/guide/lihistory/ny-history_motion_air1,0,5935662.story?coll=ny-lihistory-navigation (January 1, 2007).

23 Ibid.

26 Nancy Milford, *Savage Beauty: The Life of Edna St. Vincent Millay* (New York: Random House, 2002), 252.

26 Ibid.

27 Thomas H. White, "Broadcasting Becomes Widespread," *United States Early Radio History*, n.d. http://earlyradiohistory.us/sec018.htm (May 21, 2007).

29 Charles Joyner, "Julia Peterkin," *Carter G. Woodson Institute for African-American and African Studies at the University of Virginia*, n.d., http://www.virginia.edu/woodson/courses/hius324/peterkin.html (February 9, 2007).

29 Ibid.

29 Julia Peterkin, *Scarlet Sister Mary* (Athens: University of Georgia Press, 1998), 249.

29–30 Mead, 108.

30 Josephine Lawrence, "I Am Glad I Was Born a Woman," *Newark Sunday Call*, January 27, 1924, *Josephine Lawrence Web Page*, January 28, 2004, http://www.readseries.com/joslaw/1-27-24s.jpg (February 9, 2007).

30 Paul Geraldy, "The Marrying Age," in *The World in Vogue*, edited by Bryan Holme, Katharine Tweed, Jessica Daves, and Alexander Liberman (New York: Viking Press, 1963), 115.

31 Mead, 108.

34 William H. Chafe, *The Paradox of Change: American Women in the 20th Century* (New York: Oxford University Press, 1992), 64.

35 Anna Steese Richardson, "Your Daughter and Her Job," *Good Housekeeping*, April 1924, 213.

35 Ibid.

35 Ibid.

36 Ibid., p. 29.

36 Ibid.

36 Ibid.

40 Frank B. Gilbreth Jr. and Ernestine Gilbreth Carey, *Cheaper by the Dozen* (New York: Thomas Y. Crowell Co., 1948), 38.

41 Anna Reese Richardson, "Your Daughter and Her Job," *Good Housekeeping*, April 1924, 29.

41 Bernice Lowen, *Book of Recipes: Recipes and Instructions for Hotpoint Electric Ranges* (Chicago: Edison Electric Appliance Co., 1926), 3.

41–42 Christine Frederick, "The New Housekeeping: How It Helps the Woman Who Does Her Own Work," *Ladies' Home Journal*, September 1912, 13, 70–71.

42 Ibid.

42 Ibid.

43 Ibid.

43–44 *Good Housekeeping*, "The Way We Clean Windows," April 1924, 87.

45–46 Kim Klausner, "Worried Women: The Popularization of Scientific Motherhood in the 1920s," *Ex Posto Facto*, 1995, n.d., http://userwww.sfsu.edu/~epf/1995/mothers.html (February 9, 2007).

46   *Time*, "Care of Baby," November 30, 1925, n.d., http://www.time.com/time/magazine/article/ 0,9171,736592,00.html (January 15, 2007).

46–47 Ibid.

49   Ibid., 223, 151.

49–50 Ibid., 216.

51   Advertisement for Nairn Linoleum, *Good Housekeeping*, April 1924, 167.

51   Advertisement for Ivory Soap Flakes, *Good Housekeeping*, April 1924, 14.

55   Marilyn Kern-Foxworth, *Aunt Jemima, Uncle Ben and Rastus* (Westport, CT: Greenwood Press, 1984), 90.

60   Allen, 68.

62   *New York Times*, "Mary's Little Skirt," January 27, 1921.

62–63 Bruce Bliven, "Flapper Jane," *New Republic*, September 9, 1925, available online at *Pittsburg State University*, n.d., http://faculty.pittstate .edu/~knichols/flapperjane.html (February 9, 2007).

63   Ibid.

65   Frederic D. Schwarz, "Time Machine," *American Heritage*, n.d., http://www.americanheritage.com/ articles/magazine/ah/2000/5/2000_5_90.shtml (February 9, 2007).

65   Lois Scharf and Joan M. Jensen, *Decades of Discontent: The Women's Movement, 1920–1940* (Westport, CT: Greenwood Press, 1983), 118.

66   Bliven.

66–67 Bliven.

67   Emily Post, *Etiquette in Society, in Business, in Politics and at Home* (New York: Funk & Wagnalls, 1922), 25.

68   Allen, 80.

69   "Short Skirts," *International Herald Tribune*, 1926. http://www.iht.com/articles/2001/01/09/edold.t_15 .php (May 16, 2007).

69   "Skirt Backwash," *International Herald Tribune*, 1926. http://www.iht.com/articles/2001/02/05/ edold.2.t_0.php (May 16, 2007)

70   Ellery Rand, "Mrs. Henderson Crusades for Modesty," *New York Times*, January 31, 1926, n.d., http://select.nytimes.com/gst/abstract.html?res=F50E 15F8395D13738DDDA80B94D9405B868EF1D3 (January 15, 2007).

70   Ibid.

70   Ibid.

70   Ibid.

70   *Time*, "The White House Week," January 11, 1926, n.d., http://www.time.com/time/magazine/article/ 0,9171,728819,00.html (January 15, 2007).

71   *Washington Post*, "Finds High Heels a Benefit," June 30, 1920.

72   Allen, 70.

73   "Revues and Other Vanities: The Commodification of Fantasy in the 1920s," n.d., http.://www.assumption .edu/ahc/Vanities/default.html(May 21, 2007).

74   Anonymous, *Fascinating Womanhood, or the Art of Attracting Men* (Saint Louis: Psychology Press, 1922), viii, available online at *Harvard University Library Open Collections Program*, February 1, 2006, http:// ocp.hul.harvard.edu/ww/organizations-bureau .html (November 4, 2006).

74   Ibid., part 4, 29.

74   Ibid., part 5, 6.

75   Ibid., part 1, 33.

75   Ibid.

76   Ibid.

76   Ibid.

76   Ibid.

77   Vicki L. Ruiz, *From Out of the Shadows: Mexican Women in Twentieth-Century America* (New York: Oxford University Press, 1998), 59.

77   Ibid., 60.

77   Ibid., 69.

77   David L. Cohn, *The Good Old Days: A History of American Morals and Manners as Seen through the Sears, Roebuck Catalogs 1905 to the Present* (New York: Simon & Schuster, 1940), 116.

80   Gilbreth and Carey, 210.

81   Ibid.

81   "Edison's Famous 1914 Anti-Cigarette Memo," n.d. http://medicolegal.tripod.com/edison1914 .htm#edison-letter (May 21, 2007).

83   Mary Patrice Thaman, *Manners and Morals of the 1920s: A Survey of the Religious Press* (New York: Bookman Associates, 1934), 96.

84   John Morelli, "Candidates, Consumers, and Closers: Albert Lasker, Advertising, and American Politics, 1900–1920, paper presented at the Ohio Valley History Conference, October 22, 1999, reprinted on *H-net, Humanities and Social Studies Online*, n.d., http://www.h-net.org/~shgape/morello.html (February 9, 2007).

85   Ibid.

85   Ibid.

86   Lifebuoy soap advertisement, *Good Housekeeping*, April 1924, 107.

89   "The Story of Carnation Milk" (Seattle, WA: *Carnation Milk Products*, 1915) 3, n.d. http://scriptorium.lib.duke.edu/eaa/cookbooks/CK00 30/CK0030-03-72dpi.jpcg (April 1, 2007).

89 Marian Jane Parker, Selected Recipes and Menus for Paries, Holidays and Special Occasions, 1, n.d. http://scriptorium.lib.duke.edu/eaa/cookbooks/CK 0045/CK0045-02-72dpi.jpeg (April 1, 2007).

91 Lulu Hunt Peters, *Diet and Health, with Key to the Calories* (Chicago: Reilly and Lee Co., 1918), 4.

92 Margaret A. Lowe, *Looking Good: College Women and Body Image, 1875–1930* (Baltimore: Johns Hopkins University Press, 2003), 134.

92 Peters, 7.

93 Enid Nemy, "Fashion Was Her Pulpit," *New York Times,* January 11, 19171, 35.

93 Ibid.

94 Lowe, 146.

101 Stephen Fox, *The Mirror Makes: A History of American Advertising and Its Creators* (New York: William Morrow and Company, 1984), 94.

101 Ibid.

102 Preiss, 128,

102–103 Ibid., 137.

104 E. Azalia Hackley, *The Colored Girl Beautiful* (Kansas City, MO: Burton Pub. Co., 1916), 9–10.

104–105 Ibid.

105 Ibid., 23.

105 Ibid.

106 "Forbade His Wife to Become Modern," *New York Times,* August 18, 1923, 2.

107 Paul Morand, "Prohibition," *Eyewitness to America,* 420.

108 Kathryn Blee, "Women in the 1920s Ku Klux Klan Movement," *Feminist Studies,* Spring 1991, 57–77.

109 Ibid., 63.

110 Hazel V. Carby, "It Jus Be's Dat Way Sometime," in *Unequal Sisters,* edited by Ellen Carol DuBois and Vicki L. Ruiz (New York: Routledge, 1990), 243.

111 Kathleen M. Blee, *Women of the Klan: Racism and Gender in the 1920s* (Los Angeles: University of California Press, 1991), 101.

111 Ibid.

112 Arnetta Hill, "The Colored Woman of To-Day," *Ohio State Monitor,* April 17, 1920, 1.

112 Ibid.

113 Ralph W. Tyler, "Women Who Achieve," *Cleveland Advocate,* July 5, 1919, 8.

114 Arnetta Hill, 147.

114 Ibid.

115 *Cleveland Union,* "Women Admitted: Klu Klux Klan Changes Constitution," August 20, 1921, available online at *Ohio Historical Society,* "The African American Experience in Ohio, 1859–1920, *Ohio Historical Society,* n.d., http://dbs.ohiohistory .org/africanam/page.cfm?ID=1457&Current=01_ 02A (February 9, 2007).

115 Blee, 101.

115 Ibid., 172.

115 *Cleveland Union.*

115 "Alabama Refuses Vote to Colored Women," *Cleveland Advocate,* September 18, 1920, 4.

117 Blanche Wiesen Cook, "Eleanor Roosevelt as Reformer, Feminist, and Political Boss," *Women's America,* 371.

117 Ibid.

117 Ibid., 373.

119 Chafe, 28.

119 Roberta W. Frances, "The History Behind the Equal Rights Amendment," n.d. http://www .equalrightsamendment.org/era.htm (May 21, 2007).

120 Allen, *Only Yesterday,* 256.

122 *Los Angeles Times,* "Faithful Cling to Waning Hope," May 20, 1926, n.d., http://xroads.virginia .edu/~ug00/robertson/asm/latimes.html (February 9, 2007).

126 Margaret Sanger, "Raid on a Bird Control Clinic," April 15, 1929, *Eyewitness to History,* ed. David Colbert (New York: Vintage Books, 1998), 421.

127 Ibid., 422.

127 *Time,* "Birth Control Raid," April 29, 1929, n.d., http://www.time.com/time/magazine/article/ 0,9171,769202,00.html (January 1, 2007).

128 *Time,* "Uncensored?" September 8, 1924, n.d., http://www.time.com/time/magazine/article/ 0,9171,718988,00.html (January 1, 2007).

128 Ibid.

128–129 Carrie Chappman Catt, "Poison Propaganda," *The Woman Citizen* (31 May 1924): 14, 32–33. Accessible in Women and Social Movements in the United States, 1600–2000, n.d. http://womhist .binghamton.edu/wilpf/doc4.htm (May 21, 2007).

129 "Uncensored?"

131 Grace Abbott, "Children and the Depression: A National Study and Warning," *New York Times,* December 18, 1922, XX5.

Selected Bibliography

Allen, Frederick Lewis. *The Big Change.* New York: Harper and Brothers, 1952.

____. *Only Yesterday: An Informal History of the 1920s.* New York: Harper & Row, 1931.

Andriest, Ralph K. *The American Heritage History of the 1920s & 1930s.* New York: American Heritage Publishing Company, 1970.

Anonymous. *Fascinating Womanhood, or the Art of Attracting a Man.* Saint Louis: Psychology Press, 1922. Available online at *Harvard University Library Open Collections Program.* February 1, 2006. http:// ocp.hul.harvard.edu/ ww/organizations-bureau.html (November 4, 2006).

Ball, Christina, "The Silencing of Clara Bow," *Gadfly Online.* 2007. http://gadflyonline.com/ (April 30, 2007).

Blee, Kathleen M. *Women of the Klan: Racism and Gender in the 1920s.* Los Angeles: University of California Press, 1991.

____. "Women in the 1920s Ku Klux Klan Movement," *Feminist Studies* 17, 1991.

Bliven, Bruce. "Coney Island for Battered Souls," *New Republic,* November 23, 1921, 372–374. Available online at *Amusement Park History.* 2004. http://history .amusement-parks.com/bliven.htm (May 7, 2007).

____. "Flapper Jane." *New Republic,* September 9, 1925.

Bonner, Paul H., Jr., ed. *The World in Vogue.* New York: Viking Press, 1963.

Bow, Clara, and Adela Rogers St. Johns. "My Life Story." *Photoplay,* February–April 1928.

Boyle, Kevin. *Arc of Justice: A Saga of Race, Civil Rights, and Murder in the Jazz Age.* New York: Owl Books, 2004.

Broer, Lawrence R., and John D. Walther, eds. *Dancing Fools and Weary Blues: The Great Escape of the Twenties.* Bowling Green, OH: Bowling Green State University, 1990.

Brumberg, Joan Jacobs. "Fasting Girls: The Emerging Ideal of Slenderness in American Culture." In *Women's America: Refocusing the Past.* 4th ed. New York: Oxford University Press, 1995.

Buschka, Mary Ann. "Happiness Minutes: Technology and Psychology in the Home." *City University of New York.* 2001. http://dsc.gc.cuny.edu/part/part7/articles/ buschk.html (February 14, 2007).

Carby, Hazel V. "It Jus Be's Dat Way Sometime." *Unequal Sisters: A Multi-Cultural Reader in J. S. Women's History.* Edited by Ellen Carol DuBois and Vicki L. Ruiz. New York: Routledge, 1990.

Chafe, William H. *The Paradox of Change: American Women in the 20th Century.* New York: Oxford University Press, 1992.

Cohn, David L. *The Good Old Days: A History of American Morals and Manners as Seen through the Sears, Roebuck Catalogs 1905 to the Present.* New York: Simon & Schuster, 1940.

Cowan, Ruth Schwartz. *More Work for Mothers: The Ironies of Household Technologies from the Open Hearth to the Microwave.* New York: Basic Books, 1983.

____. "The 'Industrial Revolution' in the Home: Household Technology and Social Change in the Twentieth Century." *Women's America: Refocusing the Past.* 4th ed. New York: Oxford University Press, 1995.

Duke University. "Emergence of Advertising in America." Rare Book, Manuscript, and Special Collections Library, Duke University. Available online at *American Memory.* N.D. *Library of Congress.* http://memory.loc.gov/ ammem/award98/ncdhtml/eaahome.html (May 4, 2007).

Faulkner, Anne Shaw. "Does Jazz Put the Sin in Syncopation?" *Ladies' Home Journal,* August 1921, 16–34.

Fields, Jill. "'Fighting the Corsetless Evil': Shaping Corsets and Cultures, 1900–1930." *Journal of Social History,* Winter 1999. Available online at *findarticles.com,* n.d. http://findarticles.com/p/articles/mi_m2005/is_2_33/ai _58675450 (May 4, 2007).

Fox, Stephen. *The Mirror Makes: A History of American Advertising and Its Creators.* New York: William Morrow and Company, 1984.

Gilbreth, Frank B., Jr., and Ernestine Gilbreth Carey. *Cheaper by the Dozen:* New York: Thomas Y. Crowell Company, 1948.

Good Housekeeping, "The Way We Clean Windows," April 1924, 87.

____. "Your Daughter and Her Job," April 1924, 28.

Hackley, E. Azalia. *The Colored Girl Beautiful.* Kansas City, MO: Burton Publishing Company, 1916.

Halper, Donna L. *Invisible Stars: A Social History of Women in American Broadcasting*. New York: M. E. Sharpe, 2001.

Immerso, Michael. *Coney Island: The People's Playground*. New Brunswick, NJ: Rutgers University Press, 2002.

Kern-Foxworth, Marilyn. *Aunt Jemima, Uncle Ben and Rastus*. Westport, CT: Greenwood Press, 1984.

Klausner, Kim. "Worried Women: The Popularization of Scientific Motherhood in the 1920s." *Ex Posto Facto*. 1995. *San Francisco State University*. N.d. http://userwww.sfsu.edu/~epf/1995/mothers.html (February 9, 2007).

Lamb, Ruth de Forest. *American Chamber of Horrors*. New York: Farrar & Rinehart, 1936.

Lowe, Margaret A. *Looking Good: College Women and Body Image, 1875–1930*. Baltimore: Johns Hopkins University Press, 2003.

Lynd, Robert S., and Helen Merrell Lynd. *Middletown: A Study in Contemporary American Culture*. New York: Harcourt, Brace and Company, 1929.

Mayfield, Sara. *Exiles from Paradise: Zelda and Scott Fitzgerald*. New York: Delacorte Press, 1971.

Mead, Margaret. *Blackberry Winter: My Earlier Years*. New York: William Morrow & Co, 1972.

Milford, Nancy. *Savage Beauty: The Life of Edna St. Vincent Millay*. New York: Random House, 2002.

New York Times. "Mary's Little Skirt," June 27, 1921, 10.

____. "Y.W.C.A. Urges Shoe Reform," May 12, 1919, 13.

Nolan, Stephanie. *Promised the Moon: The Untold Story of the First Women in the Space Race*. New York: Four Walls Eight Windows, 2002.

Ohio Historical Society. "The African–American Experience in Ohio, 1850–1920." *Ohio Historical Society*. N.d. http://dbs.ohiohistory.org/africanam/index.stm (April 30, 2007).

Ohio State University. "Clash of Cultures in the 1910s and 1920s." *Harvey Goldberg Program for Excellence in Teaching, Department of History. Ohio State University*, date. http://ehistory.osu.edu/osu/mmh/clash (May 14, 2007).

Palmer, Phyllis. *Domesticity and Dirt: Housewives and Domestic Servants in the U.S., 1920–1945*. Philadelphia: Temple University Press, 1989.

Peterkin, Julia. *Scarlet Sister Mary*. Athens: University of Georgia Press, 1998.

Peters, Lulu Hunt. *Diet and Health, with Key to the Calories*. Chicago: Reilly and Lee Co., 1918.

Phillips, Dorothy Sanborn. "Wait for Me." *Good Housekeeping*, April 1924.

Post, Emily. *Etiquette in Society, in Business, in Politics and at Home*. New York: Funk & Wagnalls, 1922.

Preiss, Kathy. *Hope in a Jar: The Making of America's Beauty Culture*. New York: Henry Holt Company, 1998.

Riordan, Teresa. *Inventing Beauty*. New York: Broadway Books, 2004.

Ruiz, Vicki L. *From Out of the Shadows: Mexican Women in Twentieth-Century America*. New York: Oxford University Press, 1998.

Sanger, Margaret. "Raid of a Birth Control Clinic." In David Colbert, ed. *Eyewitness to America*. New York: Vintage Books, 1998.

Scharf, Lois, and Joan M. Jensen. *Decades of Discontent: The Women's Movement, 1920–1940*. Westport, CT: Greenwood Press, 1983.

Scranton, Philip, ed. *Beauty and Business: Commerce, Gender, and Culture in Modern America*. New York: Routledge, 2001.

Smith, Ethel M. *Towards Equal Rights for Men and Women*. Washington, DC: National League of Women Voters, 1929.

St. Johns, Adela Rogers. *Some Are Born Great*. New York: Doubleday & Co., 1974.

Thaman, Mary Patrice. *Manners and Morals of the 1920s: A Survey of the Religious Press*. New York: Bookman Associates, 1934.

Time-Life. *This Fabulous Century: Sixty Years of American Life. Volume III: 1920–1930*. New York: Time-Life Books, 1969.

U.S. Department of Labor. "Fact Finding with the Women's Bureau." Bulletin 84. Washington, D.C.: U.S. Department of Labor, Women's Bureau, March 1931.

Washington Post. "Lay the High Heels Low," May 6, 1920, 6.

Woodhead, Lindy. *War Paint: Madame Helena Rubinstein & Miss Elizabeth Arden, Their Lives, Their Times, Their Rivalry*. Hoboken, NJ: John Wiley & Sons, 2003.

Further Reading and Websites

BOOKS

Collins, Gail. *America's Women: 400 Years of Dolls, Drudges, Helpmates, and Heroines.* New York: William Morrow, 2003.

Feldman, Ruth Tenzer. *World War I.* Minneapolis: Twenty-First Century Books, 2004.

Kendall, Martha E. *Failure Is Impossible: The History of American Women's Rights.* Minneapolis: Twenty-First Century Books, 2001.

O'Neal, Michael J. *America in the 1920s.* New York: Facts on File, 2005.

Weatherly, Myra, and Helen Cothran, eds. *Living in 1920s America.* Farmington Hills, MI: Greenhaven, 2005.

Winget, Mary. *Eleanor Roosevelt.* Minneapolis: Twenty-First Century Books, 2001.

WEBSITES

Advertisements

"The Ad*Access Project" and "Medicine and Madison Avenue"
http://scriptorium.lib.duke.edu/adaccess
These two websites, both accessible through the Rare Book, Manuscript, and Special Collections Library, Duke University, offer thousands of advertisements printed in U.S. and Canadian newspapers and magazines between 1911 and 1955. The main subject categories are Beauty and Hygiene, Radio, Television, Transportation, and World War II.

Magazine Cover Art

MagazineArt.org.
http://www.magazineart.org
This site features color images from hundreds of magazines published in the nineteenth and early twentieth centuries. Also provided is information about magazines, their publishers, editors, artists, and publishing companies.

Radio and Film

Radio Days
http://www.otr.com/index.shtml
This site has a wonderful collection of articles, radio scripts, and images about radio from its earliest days through the 1950s. Topics include comedy, mystery, science fiction, and radio news.

Turner Classic Movies
http://www.tcm.com/index.jsp
TCM's online site provides useful articles on classic films and filmmakers, often with production and movie still images.

A Wireless Message
http://earlyradiohistory.us
For additional information about early radio programs and in particular the *Man in the Moon* stories, see Thomas H. White's "A Wireless Message: Articles and Extracts."

Society and Social Custom

American Women
http://memory.loc.gov/ammem/awhhtml
The site includes rare books and images as well as topics of discussion ranging from suffrage and labor to art. The site covers multiple centuries.

Clash of Cultures
http://ehistory.osu.edu/osu/mmh/clash/default.htm
This website is part of the outreach mission of the Harvey Goldberg Program for Excellence in Teaching in the Department of History at Ohio State University. The site provides topics for discussion as well as primary source articles and images about significant events and people of the 1920s.

Index

Photo Acknowledgments

The images in this book are used with the permission of: © Hulton Archive/Getty Images, pp. 3, 12, 13, 19, 20, 21, 29 (1st and 3rd from left), 33 (top), 58, 59, 61, 62, 66, 71 (top), 72, 73, 86, 93, 99, 108, 123, 126, 130; www.magazineart.org, pp. 4, 46; © Bettmann/CORBIS, pp. 6, 44, 80, 111, 116, 125; © New York Times Co./Hulton Archive/Getty Images, p. 7; Library of Congress, pp. 8 (LC-USZ62-76298), 15 (LC-USZ62-120226), 26 (LC-USZ62-42479), 29 (4th from left- LC-USZ62-137303), 65 (LC-USZC4-3274), 68 (LC-USZ62-99824), 69 (LC-USZ62-93261), 78 (LC-USZ62-106965), 88 (LC-DIG-ppmsc-05879), 119 (LC-DIG-ggbain-37403, LC-USZ62-37937), 120 (LC-DIG-ggbain-37272), 121 (LC-DIG-ggbain-29524), 129 (LC-USZ62-109793), 131 (LC-DIG-ppmsca-03054); © CORBIS, pp. 9, 55; © UnderwoodArchives.com, pp. 11, 43; © The Granger Collection, New York, pp. 17, 33 (bottom), 38, 39, 103; AP Photo, p. 18; The Cradle of Aviation Museum, p. 23; Courtesy Lilly Library, Indiana University, Bloomington, IN, pp. 24, 82; Donna Halper, p. 25; © Archive Photos/Getty Images, p. 29 (2nd from left); John W. Hartman Center for Sales, Advertising & Marketing History, Rare Book, Manuscript, and Special Collections Library, Duke University: [Ad*Access On-Line Project, pp. 32 (Ad # BH2096. Used with the permission of The Procter & Gamble Company), 48 (left Ad # BH0466), p. 94 (left, Ad # BH1219; right, Ad # BH1018), 98 (Ad # BH1359), 100 (Ad # BH0002, Copyright Kimberly-Clark Worldwide, Inc. Reprinted with Permission)], [Medicine and Madison Avenue On-Line Project. pp. 52 (Ad #MM0657, © McNEIL-PPC, Inc. 2007; Advertisement © 1920s. Used by permission), 53 (Ad #MM1128)], [Emergence of Advertising in America On-Line Project, pp. 89 (Ad #CK0030, the Cookbook Collection. This artwork is made available as a courtesy of Nestlé USA. Carnation® is a registered trademark of Société des Produits Nestlé S.A., Vevey, Switzerland), 102 (Ad #P0170. POND'S is a registered trademark of Unilever)]; LOVE'S WILDERNESS © Corinne Griffith Productions, Inc. Licensed By Warner Bros. Entertainment, Inc. All Rights Reserved, pp. 36, 74 (photos provided by The Granger Collection, New York); © Underwood & Underwood/CORBIS, p. 40; The Schlesinger Library, Radcliffe Institute, Harvard University, p. 41; Private collection, pp. 48 (right, © McNEIL-PPC, Inc. 2007; Advertisement © 1920s. Used by permission), 50 (right); www.nostalgiaville.com, p. 50 (left); © American Stock/Hulton Archive/Getty Images, p. 60; © George Hommel/John Kobal Foundation/Getty Images, p. 64; © John Kobal Foundation/Hulton Archive/Getty Images, p. 67; www.adclassix.com, p. 71 (bottom); Courtesy of the Frank and Lillian Gilbreth Papers, Purdue University Libraries, Archives and Special Collections, p. 79; © Mansell/Time & Life Pictures/Getty Images, p. 84; General Research Division, The New York Public Library, pp. 87 (all), 90; Courtesy of the Burton Historical Collection, Detroit Public Library, p. 104; © 2007 Fantagraphics Books; courtesy of Fantagraphics Books; fantagraphics.com., p. 106; Swarthmore College Peace Collection, Records of Women's International League for Peace and Freedom, p. 107; Archives Collection, Birmingham Public Library, Birmingham, AL, p. 109; Cleveland Public Library Photograph Collection, p. 112; © Hulton-Deutsch Collection/CORBIS, p. 118; Sears® Holdings Archives, p. 133.

Front cover (top): © Playboy Archive/CORBIS.

Front cover (bottom): © H. Armstrong Roberts/Retrofile/Getty Images.

About the Author

Catherine Gourley is an award-winning author and editor of books for young adults. A former editor of *Read* magazine, Gourley is the national director for Letters About Literature, a reading-writing promotion program of the Center for the Book in the Library of Congress. In addition, she is the curriculum writer for The Story of Movies, an educational outreach program on film study and visual literacy in the middle school developed by The Film Foundation, Los Angeles.

Among Gourley's more than twenty books are *Media Wizards* and *Society's Sisters* as well as the other four volumes in the Images and Issues of Women in the Twentieth Century series—*Gibson Girls and Suffragists: Perceptions of Women from 1900 to 1918*; *Rosie and Mrs. America: Perceptions of Women in the 1930s and 1940s*; *Gidgets and Women Warriors: Perceptions of Women in the 1950s and 1960s*; and *Ms. and the Material Girls: Perceptions of Women from the 1970s through the 1990s*.